FRANCESCO'S
ITALY

FRANCESCO'S
ITALY

FRANCESCO DA MOSTO

PHOTOGRAPHS BY JOHN PARKER

BOOKS

FRANCESCO'S ITALY

LAKE MAGGIORE
LAKE COMO
LAKE GARDA
VENETO
LOMBARDY
Verona
Vicenza
Milan
Cremona
Padua
Venice
Mantua
Turin
Ferrara
PIEDMONT
Bologna
EMILIA-ROMAGNA
LIGURIAN COAST
Lucca
Florence
Pisa
Urbino
San Gimignano
LE MARCHE
TUSCANY
Assisi
Siena
UMBRIA
Elba
Orvieto
LAZIO
Rome
CAMPANIA
PUGLIA
Naples
VESUVIUS
Matera
Lecce
Capri
BASILICATA
CALABRIA
Palermo
Monreale
Messina
Segesta
ETNA
SICILY
Agrigento
Syracuse
Noto

6

PREFACE

I began travelling in Italy at an early age and have been interested, ever since, in the way that expressions, dialect, architecture, culture, creativity, people too, change from place to place, even over small geographical distances. Italy is a young country that only came together 150 years ago, and before that we were a collection of hundreds of cities and states, all ruled by different people. Every town has its own character, its own customs, and often its own great artist. An Italian's loyalty lies in his home town, not in the state; yet, regional differences aside, it is this love for his 'country' that unites all Italians.

I was born in Venice – but for at least the past four generations the da Mostos have always chosen their brides from elsewhere. My mother is Sicilian. I have family in almost every part of the country, and for us Italians the family is everything: the blood of all Italy runs through my veins. This book follows a journey I have recently made across the country from top to toe, starting in Venice, where I still live, and finishing in Palermo. It was wonderful to have been given the opportunity to make this journey and, while revisiting places that are special to me, I have also loved exploring my country and discovering new marvels.

Italy is a land of stunning landscapes; its ancient streets hum with modern life, while its towns are packed with masterpieces of art and architecture. The Italian people are possessed by beauty, passion, style, and of course, food and wine. These passions seem to have no limits and we have always been keen to demonstrate this – it is said that when Charles III of France passed through Conegliano on his way to Venice, fine wine was made to flow in the fountain of the main square for two days and nights! It was enjoyed by him, his retinue and, it goes without saying, the local population.

Italy is also *il bel casino*, the great confusion. But, for all the confusion, Italy is strangely united: we have our language, our customs, our art, and, yes, perhaps we also have a unique way of seeing the world, of living our lives.

1

LEAVING THE LAGOON

WEALTH, FASHION & ROMANCE

The Veneto – Venice, Padua, Vicenza, Verona & Lake Garda;
Emilia-Romagna – Ferrara & Bologna; Lombardy – Mantua, Cremona,
Milan & Lake Como; Piedmont – Turin; the Ligurian coast

ABOVE AND OPPOSITE: Venice, my home and where my journey begins. Venetians are not usually considered to be the best drivers on the roads, but being able to navigate through the chaos of the Grand Canal should count for something.
PREVIOUS PAGE LEFT: The interior of Sant' Apollinare in Classe, Ravenna, one of the most illustrious expressions of Byzantine artistry in the world.
PREVIOUS PAGE RIGHT: Sunrise on the Venetian lagoon.

Crossing the strip of water between Venice and the mainland, which we Venetians regard in a rather detached manner, both literally and metaphorically, is a strange and contradictory experience. When we leave seawards – heading south-west, that is – we feel a sense of adventure, as if we might never return, since that immense mass of liquid, our lady and our mistress, could engulf us. However, when we set out for the calm mainland the journey is one of a different kind of discovery: we are heading for places and people that are different from us, and the greatest unknown is constituted by man rather than by nature, which has now, on the whole, been tamed.

It is no accident that the oldest roots of the pre-Roman civilization of the Veneto region are to be found in the fertile soil of the Euganean Hills. These are a cluster of volcanic cones, whose ancient heat is still released in thermal waters; long ago their natural qualities fostered the development of a flourishing community known as the Veneti. The centre of this civilization, which preceded that of Venice, was the territory of Este, which then became the Roman Ateste. The people who lived on these hillsides undoubtedly travelled to far-off lands and traded with them. However, the best-known connection between this region and other Mediterranean cultures is Antenor who, according to legend, fled here from Troy and founded the nearby city of Padua.

Long before the birth of the Most Serene Republic of Venice, a distant ancestor of my family, Titus Mustius, was a prominent citizen of Padua. The family name is said to derive from the must from which wine is fermented – a reminder, therefore, of the orgiastic festivals held in honour of Bacchus, the god of wine. These celebrations became so wild that they had to be forbidden by senatorial decree – unsurprisingly, a decree that was widely ignored.

In AD 86 Mustius is on record as having tried to intercede with the Emperor Nerva, pleading with him to 'have pity on two great Paduan women for the innocence of their ways, the exemplarity of their actions and the refinement of their memorable lives'. They had lived in exile for 36 years, after being driven out during the persecutions of Nero. Ten years earlier that infamous emperor had burned down the city of Rome, blaming it on the Christians and

accusing them of atheism because they did not worship the pagan gods and of cannibalism because they professed to eat the body of Christ. Now, in a more liberal climate, these women hoped to be allowed to return home at last.

The Euganean Hills lie south-west of Padua and are visible from the lagoon of Venice, especially in the evening when the sun sinks behind them; they rise from the plain like distant but watchful relatives. It is not difficult to understand why the medieval poet Francesco Petrarch, summoned by the ruling family, the Carraresi, to spend his old age in Padua, preferred to retire to the village of Arquà in the hills. But the peace and serenity he found in these final years did not survive the grave. In the seventeenth century a priest broke into his tomb, scavenging for relics; and recently a professor at the Polytechnic of Milan has added another element of disturbance, this time to his literary remains. By applying a mathematical model to the lyrics of Petrarch's *Canzoniere*, love poems dedicated to the object of his unrequited passion, Laura, the professor has deduced that the poet's ecstasy and despair alternated according to regular four-year cycles.

Around the time of Petrarch's birth at the beginning of the fourteenth century, the Scrovegni Chapel, one of the greatest works of Western civilization, was built in Padua. In a simple Gothic style, it follows the elliptical outlines of the remains of Padua's Roman Arena and clearly marks the beginning of Western art. The interior was enriched with frescoes that the artist Giotto was commissioned to paint by Enrico degli Scrovegni, one of Padua's richest and most powerful citizens.

Giotto's extraordinary genius can be seen in all its originality in these paintings, which cover every wall with images of the Virgin Mary, Christ, the Vices and Virtues, the Apocalypse and the Last Judgement. Previously, Christ had always been depicted as a distant figure, as for instance in the dispassionate images of icons, but Giotto wanted to portray him as a real person, who feels pain and experiences love, in a way that ordinary Italians could understand. By turning the Bible into a kind of medieval romance, Giotto changed art for ever. Every surface of the chapel bursts with colour and brilliant imagery as Giotto tells the story of Christ's life in panels, like a comic strip!

ABOVE: One of Giotto's last panels in the Scrovegni sequence, showing the deposition of Christ.

OPPOSITE: The Rocca degli Alberi, incorporated within the walls of Montagnana, south-west of Padua. The walls, made of brick and stone, are among the best conserved medieval fortifications in Europe.

First, Giotto tells of the Virgin Mary's birth, her conception sealed by a passionate kiss between her parents. Then he shows how Joseph competes with other men to win Mary's hand. By emphasizing the love between Mary's parents and between Mary and Joseph, the artist makes the point that Christ is not just the son of God but a child born of love. Every stage is full of emotion and drama: anguish as mothers shed tears, the first in Western painting; brutality in the Massacre of the Innocents; anger as Christ throws the moneylenders out of the Temple; betrayal as Judas embraces the Messiah he has sold to the authorities; bitter humiliation as Christ is abused at the hands of Pilate's guards. By the time he is crucified, Christ is a frail, broken man and his death tears at the hearts of those who love him.

SINCE TIME IMMEMORIAL the backbone of Italy, formed by the Apennine range, has given inhabitants the opportunity to build easily defensible strongpoints. Montagnana, a few kilometres west of Este, became a stronghold originally for the defence of Ravenna against invaders from the north in the fifth century AD, and then later for the Lombards as the border of the territories controlled by the Eastern Empire from Byzantium. The early fortifications consisted of ramparts, palisades, ditches and barriers of thorny plants, reinforced in the tenth century during the incursions of the Magyars. Throughout the Middle Ages Montagnana continued to protect the neighbouring villages, whose inhabitants were under feudal obligation to maintain the fortress and to present themselves for military service. As a fortified border post, it was of vital importance in the continual squabbles between the communes of Padua, Verona and Vicenza, which were typical of the dynastic power struggles of medieval Italy.

In 1242 Ezzelino III da Romano, under the auspices of the Emperor Frederick II, took possession of Padua and Montagnana, burning the latter down and then rebuilding its fortifications. These stupendous walls had a circumference of nearly 2 kilometres, punctuated by a series of 24 towers. After this time Montagnana was drawn into the orbit of Padua as an outpost against Verona. The lords of Verona, the Scaligeri, subdued Montagnana but then lost it to the Carraresi of Padua. The latter strengthened the fortified outer walls, and added the Rocca (Castle) degli Alberi. The Carraresi dynasty came to a dramatic end when its head and his two sons were tried by the Venetian authorities for treason, sabotage and corruption and were

THE FORTRESS OF MONTAGNANA

strangled in Venice's prisons, the notorious *pozzi*, in 1406. At this point Montagnana came under Venetian rule.

Although Ezzelino's fortifications were rendered inadequate by the firepower of modern artillery, the medieval walls of Montagnana maintained their strategic importance over the centuries. The sight of these walls, which have remained intact to the present day, starts my mind thinking of those still moments in history, those occasional pauses between conflicts. It brings to mind the atmosphere of Dino Buzzati's novel *The Desert of the Tartars*, in which the absurd becomes the normal, death becomes a character, and loneliness both divides and joins together humanity. It was published just as Italy was becoming involved in the second of the two most terrible wars of the twentieth century.

Buzzati was born at the beginning of the century near Belluno. His own particular universe, in which reality and imagination were inextricably mingled, can be traced back to his childhood in

the family villa, which had a library and a barn haunted by the ghost of an old bailiff. After military service in 1928 he joined the Milan newspaper *Corriere della Sera*, where he worked until his death. In 1939 the newspaper sent him to Ethiopia as a special correspondent; a year later Buzzati became a war correspondent and published this novel, halfway between comedy and tragedy.

The solid, unchanging walls of Montagnana remind me of the fortress in *The Desert of the Tartars*: a border outpost on the edge of a desert, once attacked by the Tartars and now regulated by strict discipline. Those who live there fall under a kind of spell that renders them unable to abandon the fortress, where time and circumstances are stronger than anyone's will.

The main protagonist of the novel, Giovanni Drogo, just 21 years old, arrives at the fortress confident that he will be leaving shortly, but he too soon falls under its spell. Self-assured and knowing that he has his whole life stretching before him, he has no doubt that his great opportunity is waiting just around the corner. The soldiers are all sustained by one great hope: to see the Tartars arrive so that they can fight, win glory and become heroes. And so Giovanni falls in with the routine, giving himself up to the reassuring regularity of military discipline. Fifteen years go by before he realizes that time is passing, and with it his youth. The soldiers' lives are frittered away in this sterile, futile idleness. And when the Tartars finally do attack, Drogo, now a sick man, is obliged to leave the fortress to go and die all alone in an anonymous rented room in the city, 'an exile among strangers'.

THE VILLAS OF THE BRENTA CANAL

IN 1345, WHEN A LAW forbidding Venetian citizens to purchase land on the mainland was repealed, rich patricians started to move to the country-side along the banks of the River Brenta, which at this time was being canalized to deal with the problems of flooding on the mainland and the build-up of silt in the lagoon. This was the origin of the *Ville Venete*, part farms, part summer residences, that stretch along the canal linking Venice with Padua like an extension of the Grand Canal, with over 70 luxurious villas adorning its banks. In 1697 the geographer Vincenzo Coronelli described it in these words: 'The banks on both sides of this river are full of palaces and the delightful residences of noble-men and the most opulent citizens, with orchards, gardens and well-populated villages.'

The Venetian playwright Carlo Goldoni observed: 'Everyone enjoys immense freedom, there are games, gambling, dancing and spectacles.' The privileged set out from Venice in comfortable boats called *burchielli*, which were rowed across the lagoon and then along the Riviera del Brenta, drawn by horses along the towpath. The journey was fascinating and enjoyable: 'A river,' as Gabriele d'Annunzio wrote in his novel *Il Fuoco* (*Fire*), 'that was once magnificent and glorious in the sonnets of amorous priests, when the *burchielli* used to float along it filled with music and other pleasures.'

The Riviera del Brenta was mentioned by Dante in his *Divine Comedy*; it was visited by Casanova, Galileo and Byron, painted by Tiepolo and Canaletto, praised by Goethe and Goldoni; it hosted royalty of France and Russia, Napoleon, the Habsburgs and the house of Savoy.

OPPOSITE ABOVE: The Villa Pisani at Strà.
OPPOSITE BELOW: A detail of one of the caryatids holding up the main portico on the Riviera facade.
LEFT: Palladio's Villa Foscari at Malcontenta.

One of the first villas along the canal from Venice is the Villa Foscari at Malcontenta, one of Palladio's masterpieces. The name 'Malcontenta' possibly derives from a member of the Foscari family who was locked up in the villa on account of her promiscuous ways. Her ghost, that of a striking red-haired woman, is said to haunt the gardens and the villa, still a prisoner to her own sins; her portrait, as a lady in a red dress with a high lace collar, has been identified in one of the frescoes. However, others claim that the name alludes to the war against Venice, when the Paduans diverted the course of the Brenta Canal and caused it to flood. It was then known as the Canal of the Malcontents, and the name was supposedly passed on to both village and villa.

Raised on a podium like a classical temple, it is strongly reminiscent of the buildings of ancient Rome. As in Venice, the main façade looks towards the water so that it is mirrored in the canal, and two majestic flights of steps provide a ceremonial entrance for visitors who would disembark in front of the building.

Palladio, while always careful to include such functional details as stables, cellars and gran-aries for his villas, was too early in history to accommodate other domestic facilities that we now take for granted. At that time the custom was to provide a 'commode' on the staircase landings. There was little privacy. The 'room' consisted of two niches, with two seats facing one another, on the landing; a screen hid the area when it was empty, but lack of space meant that it had to remain open if anyone was sitting there. When using the commode one could preserve one's dignity by wearing long clothes and a mask, which was kept hanging on a nail in the niche, to provide at least an illusion of anonymity. When matters had been concluded, a servant would come to remove the results to the dung-heap. During the holiday season groups of merry-makers would go partying from one villa to another, and the local peasants greatly appreciated the contributions made to their stock of natural fertilizers.

Continuing towards Padua, near the town of Mira sits the Villa Corner, which used to host grand receptions that went on for eight days at a time. Further on is the Villa Foscarini, where Byron stayed during the summers of 1817 and 1818 while writing the fourth Canto of *Childe Harold's Pilgrimage*. He brought with him luxurious furnishings, horses for his afternoon rides and Marianna Segati, the dark-eyed wife of a cloth merchant and his first Venetian love. She was, however, soon replaced by the wife of a local baker, whom Byron then took back to Venice. Jealous and violent, the *Fornarina* (baker-woman) exhausted the poet. He had considerable difficulty sending her back home: there were furious scenes and the lady had to be fished out of the canal into which she had dived in despair.

The grandest villa on the Riviera is the Villa Pisani at Strà – mainland palace of the doges, built in the eighteenth century as a status symbol by Alvise, the first of the Venetian Pisani family to achieve that high office. This villa is nothing more nor less than a royal palace. The façade is decked out with grandiose statues, and the interior was decorated by leading Venetian artists of the times, notably Rosalba Carriera, Guarana and Tiepolo, the last of whom painted the ceiling fresco in the ballroom glorifying the Pisani family.

In front of the villa, on the other side of a long pool, lie the stables in an impressive theatrical building arranged in a long curve inspired by Vitruvian principles. The park of the Villa Pisani contains a number of Baroque constructions including towers, portals and an exedra – a semicircular seating arrangement designed as a viewpoint. The exedra acts as a hub for a range of carefully designed prospects, with views of the orangery, the ice-house, the various groups of statuary and the gates of the outer walls. The maze is a symbolic feature; its little tower leads to a statue of Minerva and alludes to a ritual quest for wisdom. In the eighteenth century the maze was the centre of an erotic pastime; women were pursued along its twisting paths in a game of mounting excitement, and the temple became the site of notorious passionate encounters.

Towards the end of the eighteenth century the Pisani played host to many royal visitors including Maria Elizabeth of Austria, sister of the Emperor Josef II, and the heirs of Catherine the Great of Russia. The Russian Grand Dukes made a terrible impression on their visit to Italy, squabbling over bills, spending parsimoniously and doling out miserly tips. The Pisani, on the other hand, were lavish to a fault. In 1784, when King Gustav III of Sweden was their guest, the celebrations amounted to 1,440,000 lire. To get an idea of what this sum was worth, the whole villa was sold in 1806 to Napoleon for 1,901,000 lire. It seems, however, that the French emperor only spent one night at the place, in November the following year.

The canal proceeds at a leisurely pace towards Padua, with the old lock of the Porte Contarine leading into the heart of this old river port. Here, in a quieter age, boats from the lagoon of Venice would moor alongside the old sixteenth-century walls and the great ramparts.

PALLADIO'S CITY

Journeying north of the plain of the River Po, which in Roman times was covered by thick forest, the landscape around Vicenza is marked by gently rolling hills dotted with the villas of local aristocracy. At the foot of the Berici Hills west of Padua, at the confluence of two rivers, lies this elegant town that today is known as 'Palladio's city'. Founded by the Veneti in the eighth century BC, Vicenza became a Roman 'municipium' in 49 BC. Like the other cities of the Po plain it suffered invasions of barbarian tribes – the Eruli, the Ostrogoths and the Visigoths – but with the arrival of the Lombards and then Charlemagne in AD 773 it became prosperous. By the twelfth century Vicenza was a free commune with its own consuls and an increasingly influential middle class. In the thirteenth century it was subdued first by the Emperor Frederick II, known as Barbarossa because of his red beard, and then by various ambitious local rulers: the Carraresi of Padua, the Scaligeri of Verona and the Visconti of Milan. Eventually in the early 1400s the city made an Act of Submission to Venice and it was while under Venetian dominion that it acquired architectural characteristics that would earn it the sobriquet of the 'mainland Venice'.

Nearly everything here was built or inspired by the brilliant Andrea Palladio in the sixteenth century, and it gave him the opportunity to demonstrate that he was the greatest architect of the age. The city has remained Palladian in aspect, developing in accordance with the ideals of the Renaissance. At its centre is the Piazza dei Signori, a meeting-place for its citizens, and one of Palladio's greatest achievements – the Basilica. The original medieval building was reshaped by him in the sixteenth century, when he cleverly added columns, pillars

and colonnades to buttress the failing structure. Opposite stands the unfinished Loggia del Capitanio. Elsewhere other architectural treasures can be found, including the Palazzo Barbaran da Porto; the Palazzo Chiericati, which displays Palladio's characteristic harmonious balance of solids and hollows; the Palazzo Valmarana; the Loggetta Palladiana in the Giardini Salvi, with its dedication to laughter and cheerfulness inscribed over the entrance; and a little jewel made of wood, the Teatro Olimpico. It was Palladio who designed the great palaces and façades with which the citizens of Vicenza flaunted their wealth and power to the rest of Italy. Sometimes I wonder whether Palladio was too good: his architecture was supposed to show off Vicenza, but it was so widely admired and copied that many forgot the little town of its origin.

Born in 1508 into a family of modest means in Padua, Palladio became an apprentice stonemason at the age of 13. His natural genius, especially his ability to take what was magnificent from Roman and Greek architecture and apply it tastefully and playfully to the homes of country gentlemen, was spotted very early.

Perhaps the best-known Palladian villa is the Rotonda on the outskirts of Vicenza; even its creator, in his *Four Books of Architecture*, placed this magnificent building among the palazzi and not the villas. The Villa Rotonda inspired homes built by Britain's aristocracy for centuries.

ABOVE: The Villa Rotonda, near Vicenza, is probably the most famous Palladian villa. Inspiration from the Pantheon in Rome is evident in its design, while the villa itself has inspired the creation of many others, notably Chiswick House in west London.

Paolo Almerico, for whom Palladio designed the villa in 1566, had returned to Vicenza after a brilliant career at the papal court. Of more than 20 country villas built by Palladio, this one is unusual since it has no truly practical function: it is not a farm, nor even a house to live in, but a pavilion devoted to pleasure. Almerico simply wanted a peaceful place for meditation and study and a showpiece, its purpose to please the eye with its great porticos and dome and to be a monument to its owner. This exemplifies how Palladio's villas seem to be love letters to his clients. I think he understood that when a rich client commissions his architect to design a house he doesn't necessarily want a building to live in but one that confers prestige on him, showcasing his tastes and his concept of beauty.

What makes the Rotonda unique is that it looks more like a Roman temple than a house; it is an abstraction, reflecting a superior order and harmony. Its four corners are oriented towards the four compass points, and it combines in its volume both the cube and the sphere, almost as if it were evoking the Platonic universe. Palladio thought that porticos, columns and domes, architectural elements that we associate with temples, gave magnificence and grandeur to a building, so he made them the central features of his villas. It was clearly inspired by the Pantheon of ancient Rome; the echoes of Roman civilization can be found in the simple geometric shapes and forms, which create a structure that is inherently pleasing to the eye.

The Rotonda stands alone at the top of a small hill, and Palladio exploited to the full the symmetries and forms of the gently curving mound. He succeeded in creating an icon of monumentality, an ideal model for all his architecture. It has no front or back, being exactly the same on all four sides. Palladio claimed that he gave it four porticos so that those inside could enjoy the spectacular panorama on all directions. The reverse was nearer the truth: the architect knew that every side of the villa would be visible from the surrounding countryside, and he wanted it always to be seen at its best.

WAR, VIOLENCE AND UNDYING LOVE

There is a story that a wealthy Veronese gentleman, condemned to death for a crime, was willing to pay any price to save his life. He was told he would be spared if he could build an immense amphitheatre in a single night. The man sought the help of the devil who, in exchange for his soul, promised to build it between the Ave Maria of the evening and that of the morning. All the demons came up from hell and began noisily heaping stone upon stone. The enterprise was nearing completion when the first note of the morning Ave Maria was heard and all the demons fled back to the underworld, leaving the great Arena, famous today for its stupendous operatic productions, with an incomplete outer ring.

The traces of the city's first contact with Rome, under whose rule the Arena was built to provide entertainment of a more savage kind, in fact go back to the fourth century BC, when

commercial contact between the two places was established. By 216 BC relations were on such a firm footing that the local people were recorded as having 'participated with their own contingent in the battle of Cannae' – to no avail, it would seem, since Hannibal, the invader from North Africa, dealt the Romans and their allies a resounding defeat. When the Roman Empire of the West was beginning to break up as a result of constant onslaughts from barbarian tribes from central and eastern Europe, Verona became a target for the invaders from beyond the Alps, including in the following century the Lombards, who descended into

Italy from Pannonia, present-day Hungary, with a horde of almost half a million followers seeking more fertile land. This incursion marked the beginning of two centuries of dominion over the Italian peninsula, which became one vast battlefield in the struggles between the Lombards, the Franks, the papal forces and the Roman Empire of the East, which was based in Constantinople.

Verona itself is now better known for a different sort of warring – the feuds between families that provide the background to one of the world's greatest and most tragic love stories. Thanks to William Shakespeare and his play *Romeo and Juliet*, Verona became known as the city of love. Shakespeare never actually visited the place and knew it only through Italian writers – he based his story of 'two star-crossed lovers' on an English translation of a French translation of an Italian story that was a variation of an earlier Italian story, which in its turn was based upon a fifteenth-century original. So needless to say a good deal got mislaid, if not lost, in translation.

Who were the real Romeo and Juliet? They were probably pure fiction. But does it matter? Verona is a city where you feel these events could have taken place, and that's what counts. We all want to believe that in the centre of the city the house where Juliet lived still stands. It has become a shrine for lovers and we happily imagine that the balcony, built in 1935, was the setting for Romeo's famous serenades. Shakespeare's love is fully reciprocated by the inhabitants of Verona: at one of the gates of the city, near the Arena, there is a plaque bearing Romeo's words:

> *There is no world without Verona walls,*
> *But purgatory, torture, hell itself.*
> *Hence-banished is banish'd from the world,*
> *And world's exile is death: then banished,*
> *Is death mis-term'd: calling death banishment,*
> *Thou cutt'st my head off with a golden axe,*
> *And smilest upon the stroke that murders me.*

Even if Shakespeare never came to Verona himself surely he set his greatest love story here because Italy was – and is – the country of love. Here we express what we feel. We even have a daily ritual devoted to strutting our stuff and attracting the attention of the opposite sex: in the evening we like to dress up in our finest clothes and walk up and down the main street for an hour. The smaller the town, the greater the participation. It is called the *passeggiata* or, in the south, *lo struscio*. We are out to display ourselves and, most of all, to look at others. We are a nation of voyeurs. If we see something or someone we like, we say so. And if there's no reaction, *pazienza*, no matter, we try again.

OPPOSITE: Scaligero Castle at Sirmione dates back to the thirteenth century. It sits on a peninsula that extends into Lake Garda at its southern end.

22

LAKE GARDA: SWAGGER AND SECRECY

This, the largest of the Italian lakes, lies west of Verona. It was once the border between the rival powers of Milan and Venice who fought long over it, keeping naval fleets on its waters. Bortolomio da Mosto, another ancestor of mine, was Venetian governor of this region in the sixteenth century, which meant collecting taxes and taking charge of the occupying military forces, so he probably wasn't too popular.

The shores of Lake Garda enjoy a mild climate, which favours the cultivation of olives, citrus fruits and vines; there is also something about the lake that inspires decadence. Is it the beauty of the scenery, the invigorating breeze, or the sense of solitude that seems to bring out a taste for excess? In Roman times, the wealthy built their villas along the shore. And it is here that the first-century BC poet Catullus lived, praising his little promontory as the 'gem of all peninsulas'. His rapturous, erotic poems to his mistress, Lesbia, contain all of love's emotions, ranging from passion to regret and from jealousy to obscenity.

> *Give me a thousand kisses, then a hundred*
> *Then another thousand, then a second hundred;*
> *Then yet another thousand, then a hundred;*
> *Then, when we've made many thousands,*
> *We'll confuse them all so as not to know how many.*

Two thousand years later another poet made his home here on the lake: the eccentric (and egocentric) Gabriele d'Annunzio. A great lover, he was involved with hundreds of women including, notably, the actress Eleonora Duse, but only truly loved one person: himself. When he acquired his estate in the 1920s as a gift from Italy's new ruler, Mussolini, he created a shrine to himself, which he called 'Il Vittoriale degli Italiani'. D'Annunzio also built an enormous Roman amphitheatre overlooking the lake, where his plays were performed, and a vast mausoleum was commissioned to house his remains after his death.

D'Annunzio was by now in late middle age and pleased with his life's achievements. As well as being at

that time Italy's most famous writer he had been, despite his years, a fighter pilot, a hero of World War I. In 1919 he and a small band of black-shirted fellow-adventurers had occupied the Adriatic part of Fiume which, in the aftermath of war had, to the outrage of Italians, been handed to the new state of Yugoslavia. To commemorate his patriotic if bizarre action d'Annunzio had part of the battleship used by his little invasion force installed in his sloping garden. I recall that when I was about ten, I couldn't understand why a ship had been stuck halfway up a hillside. Wasn't a ship supposed to be on water?

The hallway of d'Annuzio's house ends with doors into two rooms. The one on the left leads into a room for friends; the one on the right is for formal guests or strangers. D'Annunzio habitually made his visitors wait for up to eight hours before he deigned to see them, so the contents of the hallway include a great number of books and a gramophone to help pass the time.

He considered himself important and, for us Italians, he was. D'Annunzio was responsible for the rebirth of Italian patriotism, and is regarded as the godfather of Fascism. But when Mussolini paid a visit in 1925, he was made to wait for more than two hours in a room where d'Annunzio had placed this inscription above the mirror: 'Remember you are glass set against steel.'

Relations between the two men were problematic. Mussolini had drunk deeply of d'Annunzio's philosophy, even adopting the Roman salute and black shirts for his followers. And yet he had denied him a post within his Fascist regime. D'Annunzio's flamboyance – his boasts, for instance, that he ate dead babies – were good publicity for a poet but not for a government. Mussolini effectively kept d'Annunzio prisoner here on Lake Garda, bribing him with vast amounts of state money but never allowing him to return to public life.

In his 'gilded exile', d'Annunzio called his bedroom the Prisoner's Room, and I often wonder how he ever found time to leave it. In this house lived his principal lover and his French housekeeper, also a lover. His wife was kept in a little villa next door. Then there was also a steady flow of young women passing through; not bad for a man in his sixties. 'Woman is a science,' d'Annunzio wrote. 'A woman attracts me by what is inexplicable in her, by an indefinable knot to be undone, by an indefinable tangle to be unravelled, and especially by the particularity of her figure, by the riddle of her form, by the imports of her airs, her gestures, her attitudes.' He thought of this lakeside house as his last masterpiece, a 'book in stone'. Everything here has some connection to his life and his self-obsessed mind.

During World War II Lake Garda achieved fame once again – or, perhaps, infamy – as the part of Italy where Mussolini formed his last government: the Republic of Salò. He was by now just a puppet in the hands of the Nazis. And in these last two years of his life, legends spread of atrocious orgies held by his Fascist aides. But Lake Garda conceals another great mystery: was there a secret exchange of letters between Benito Mussolini and Winston Churchill?

THE MUSSOLINI–CHURCHILL CORRESPONDENCE

IN SEPTEMBER 1945, just after World War II had ended, the British statesman undertook the first of a series of journeys in the 'lake district' of northern Italy with his daughter Sarah. He was travelling under the assumed name of 'Colonel Waltham', supposedly on a short painting holiday. But even at the time there were rumours of private correspondence between Churchill and Mussolini, and it was suggested that he had come to Italy in the hope of retrieving papers that might prove compromising.

Churchill stayed first on Lake Como in the Villa Apraxim di Moltrasio, following the last traces of the dictator before and after his capture. Later, in July 1949, he stayed on Lake Garda near Villa Fiordaliso, the former residence of Claretta Petacci, Il Duce's lover and confidante. Here he met the carpenter who had built water-proof chests to conserve documents, which had then been thrown into the lake. He also tried to meet with one of the leaders of the Fascist secret service, to whom Mussolini was supposed to have entrusted a copy of the correspondence.

The secret services and diplomats, including the British ambassador to Italy, organized operations to get hold of Mussolini's papers. The British

26

secret service stated before the end of the war : 'Since part of the material could be compromising for the Allied governments and for certain high-ranking Italian personalities, it is in the interest of the Allies to secure the archives.'

But we need to go back a few years. In May 1940 Churchill had recently become Prime Minister. Poland, Denmark, Norway, Belgium and Holland had been invaded by Hitler, and in France the French and British armies were on the point of being surrounded. It seemed that Nazism might triumph, and many claim that secret contact had been made with Rome to try to keep Italy out of the war. According to others, however, the British and the French had asked Mussolini to enter the war so that when the armistice was signed he would be able to help persuade Hitler to moderate his demands from the defeated nations. In either case Mussolini would have been promised some kind of territorial recompense, especially in Africa.

But a few years later when Britain, with the help of the United States, was on the point of winning the war, power-relations were very different. The promises made earlier began to embarrass those who had made them – in particular, Churchill. It was now Mussolini who planned to use them to negotiate favourable peace terms.

Between autumn 1943 and April 1945 Mussolini lived on Lake Garda in the Villa Feltrinelli. It appears that in the last few months of his life he

tried to carry out secret negotiations with the British, meeting their agents near the Swiss border. On the evening of 25 April 1945, as he set out for Como, his attendant recounted:

Mussolini called me and, with a serious expression, he opened a desk drawer and pulled out a light-brown leather bag, with a zip and no handle; I recognised it at once as the same bag he had had with him during the two evenings of the meetings with the English emissaries at Porto Ceresio; he said these precise words: 'Carradori, you can abandon everything except this bag. This contains the destiny of Italy.'

This was repeated two days later after his arrest, when Il Duce told a certain partisan known as Bill: 'These documents are very important for the future of Italy.' They consisted of 160 letters from the Churchill–Mussolini correspondence – rough copies of the dictator's letters and the originals of Churchill's; in another package were political, military and diplomatic documents concerning the war in Africa, the war in Spain, the Anglo–Italian agreements made secretly in Zurich to transfer the former French colonies to Italy, the draft for future British recognition of the Italian Fascist regime, and papers about the Stresa Conference of 1935 and the Munich Agreement of 1938.

In the meantime photographic copies of the documents were circulated. The letter-headings, logos, borders, stamps and signatures were

recognized as authentic. One letter was shown to Churchill, who declared it extremely interesting but a forgery. At the same time a spokesman declared officially that 'all rumours about an exchange of letters are entirely baseless'.

At the end of the war, British secret service agents looked for documents: the Villa Feltrinelli was searched and a long list of the papers found there was made. It is now in London in the State Archive at Kew. It seems that other copies of the Churchill–Mussolini correspondence existed: one came into the hands of the monks of the monastery of St Anthony in Padua; from there it appears to have passed either to the Vatican or to Count Vittore Cini, a Venetian benefactor of the Basilica of St Anthony. Another copy seems to have been entrusted to the Japanese ambassador, Baron Shinrokuro Hidaka, and it is reasonable to suppose that one or more found its way to Germany, and it would have fallen into the hands either of the British or the Russians after the fall of the Reich. Yet another went to the last king of Italy, Umberto II, who before going into exile handed a part of it to an army major. One thing only is certain: that 60 years on, it remains one of the continuing secrets of World War II.

OPPOSITE: Lake Garda at sunset.
ABOVE: A bedroom (LEFT) and bathroom (RIGHT) in d'Annunzio's house at Il Vittoriale. Touring his dark and cluttered home, one also enters his distorted mind.

BEYOND THE RIVER PO

Any journey from northern Europe to Rome involves crossing one major natural barrier: the River Po. Many centuries before I travelled here, Christians faithfully making their pilgrimage to Rome had to cross it. Until the eighth century everyone had the right to cross the river for free – on condition that if they fell into the water their goods would go to the boatman. So the ferrymen would always let the richest pilgrims on to their boats first; the others had to wait their turn patiently. But around that time there was a change in the climate, and owing to a record drought a certain Signor Bruno from a small village near Mantua was able to fulfill his lifelong dream of crossing the River Po on foot, from the Lombardy bank to the Veneto bank. At 1.8 metres, a tall man, especially for those times, he just managed to wade across.

A little south-west of where the waters of the Po flow into the Adriatic via a marshy delta lies the city of Ferrara. In autumn and winter the city often appears like a dream in the fog, with muffled-up girls emerging from the mist on their bicycles, and the red bricks of the houses and the Castello Estense, the ducal castle, penetrating the haze. The ruling Este family of Ferrara appears to have earned its ducal title thanks to a connection with the papacy. The Marchesi d'Este were recognized as the lords of Ferrara in 1264 and became dukes following a Papal Bull of 1471. This declared that the feudal relationship between them and the Pope would cease to exist if ever there was no legitimate heir, and indeed it happened in the sixteenth century when Alfonso II failed to produce an heir despite three marriages. The papacy then took control of Ferrara and let it decay.

As the son of Alfonso I and that great, if ill-reputed, patron of the arts Lucrezia Borgia, this last Este ruler had other passions. He loved music, for instance, so intensely that he spent as much on singers and instrumentalists as he did to maintain his army of mercenaries. Lucrezia, his mother, born in 1480, had a highly colourful and scandal-ridden life among the ruthless dynastic power struggles of Renaissance Italy. The blonde-haired, blue-eyed daughter of Rodrigo Borgia, who became Pope Alexander VI, she was educated in a convent and then entrusted to the care of a cousin of the Pope. By the way, the cousin's daughter-in-law, Giulia Farnese, was the Pope's lover. When Lucrezia was 13 she was betrothed to Giovanni Sforza, the lord of Pesaro, in order to consolidate the alliance with the house of Sforza, powerful members of which had connived assiduously to ensure that Rodrigo became pope. When a plague broke out the Pope gave orders that Lucrezia, her husband and Giulia Farnese should leave Rome for Pesaro. But Giovanni Sforza stayed away longer than Lucrezia, and when he eventually turned up in Rome to reclaim her, the Borgias accused him of being a husband in name only and not in deed. He responded by accusing Lucrezia of being the incestuous lover of both her father and her brother; she was then examined and declared *virgo intacta*, whereupon the marriage was annulled.

At this point Lucrezia retired to a convent where she is said to have given birth to a child, who became known as *Infans Romanus*. According to some accounts it was her father's child,

PAGE 28: Within the sublime, pink marble walls of the octagonal Baptistry at Parma, near Mantua, the dome is divided into 16 segments, with paintings and statues depicting various stories and sequences in concentric circles, including the life of St John the Baptist and the Apostles.
PAGE 29: The Teatro all'Antica, designed by Scamozzi, is just one of the exquisite buildings created in Sabbioneta, near Mantua, as part of the poetic dream of the Renaissance soldier-prince, Vespasiano Gonzaga.
OPPOSITE: The River Po, shrouded in characteristically mysterious fog, with snow on the banks.

OPPOSITE: The cathedral in Ferrara was inaugurated in 1135 but the marble façade was remodelled in the thirteenth century. The uppermost part of the pediment depicts an interpretation of the last judgement with graphic differences between heaven and hell. St George and the dragon feature in the lunette above the main entrance.

while others claim it was her brother Cesare's; yet other sources assert that the infant wasn't Lucrezia's son at all, but one of the many bastard offspring of the Pope and his lover Giulia Farnese. In the meantime Lucrezia had fallen in love and had an affair with one of her father's chamberlains – who was later found dead in the River Tiber, tied hand and foot.

In 1498 Lucrezia was married to Alfonso of Aragon, a relative of King Alfonso of Naples. But this relationship too ended tragically. Lucrezia's ambitious brother Cesare, who had been rejected by Carlotta of Aragon and then became the cousin by marriage of King Louis XII of France, agreed to help Louis reconquer the kingdom of Naples from the Spanish, who had taken it from the French in 1442. In exchange, he wanted assistance in conquering Romagna for himself. This alliance with France alarmed Alfonso of Aragon; he first fled to his relatives – abandoning Lucrezia, who was pregnant – and then returned to Rome, where he was murdered in Lucrezia's rooms by a hired assassin of Cesare's. The official version was that Alfonso had died from a fall.

The Borgia family's subsequent matrimonial plans – that Lucrezia should marry Alfonso d'Este, the first son of Duke Ercole I – were not particularly well received by the Este family. And who could blame them? After all, the blushing 22-year-old bride did have the unfortunate reputation of being the daughter, lover and 'daughter-in-law' of Pope Alexander VI. Nonetheless on 30 December 1501 the marriage was duly celebrated in the Vatican by proxy, even though Alfonso, nervous about binding himself to a woman with such a background, had wanted to see her in person before the wedding – an unusual request in those times when high-born women were treated as political pawns to be manipulated by their families. The Este family was represented by Alfonso's three brothers who afterwards escorted Lucrezia back to Ferrara, where she was given a festive welcome despite the rumours that surrounded her.

The new bride settled down unexpectedly well in Ferrara. She continued to protect and finance her brother until their father's death, after which Cesare's ambitions were constantly thwarted by the new Pope, Julius II, formerly Giuliano della Rovere, who had been a bitter enemy of his predecessor.

Lucrezia also managed to win the respect, if not the love, of her husband. The eventual mother of seven children (three died at birth), she was prudent and patient with her father-in-law, Duke Ercole I, and eventually became Duchess of Ferrara. She established relations with members of other ruling families and with artists and writers of the age, such as the poet Ariosto and the painter Titian. At this time the duchy enjoyed a kind of golden age both politically and culturally, with flourishing schools of painting, music, theatre and poetry.

The perfect Renaissance chatelaine, this Borgia lady, whom history has so much maligned, lived for 17 years in Ferrara, loved by her family and subjects, a faithful wife and mother and a devout Christian. Nevertheless bad reputations die hard, and there was a rumour that she also had a brief flirtation with her brother-in-law Francesco Gonzaga, Duke of Mantua.

BELOW: The seventeenth-century anatomical theatre of Bologna University. Its wood panelling is animated by carved figures, including 'masters of medicine' in the niches and the notorious 'skinned ones' supporting the professor's balcony.
OPPOSITE: A trattoria in Mantua, which is famous for its delicious cuisine, especially pumpkin tortellini.

But in Ferrara, where her conduct was relatively impeccable, she was universally mourned when she died at the early age of 39, in her eighth pregnancy. She was laid to rest in the Convent of Corpus Domini.

BOLOGNA: WIDENING THE BOUNDS OF HUMAN KNOWLEDGE

Bustling streets and packed cafés, plus a large student population thanks to the university, make Bologna, south-west of Ferrara, one of Italy's most vibrant cities. Founded in 1088, the great academic institution at its heart is the oldest university in the world, famous over the centuries for its work in science and medicine.

This was the first university to practise human dissection and something very medieval still exists here: a collection of human skulls from all over Italy is housed in the entrance to the anatomy faculty. Learned men were trying to discover the secrets of human life, a journey of discovery greater even than putting man on the moon. The dissection theatre, built entirely from wood, dates from 1637. The issue of obtaining bodies to practise upon was partly solved by the fact that the Ospedale della Morte, the Hospital of Death, stood next door. A secret door between the two buildings allowed nurses to offer unclaimed bodies to the students. But the greatest problem was the Catholic Church, which feared that these doctors were trying to play God. From behind secret doors the Inquisition watched the dissections, and frequently called them to a halt. Religion was no ally to those who wished to expand the frontiers of medicine and thus help their fellow-men.

A hundred years later a sculptor called Ercole Lelli came up with a solution to providing medical students with direct experience of the human body. He fashioned two statues known as *gli spellati*, 'the skinned ones', out of wood. A versatile artist, he not only sculpted the bodies, which he called Adam and Eve, but also designed their beautiful cabinets. They turned out so well that his work continued and in the 1740s he created eight life-size anatomical models out of wax: somewhat disturbingly, the wax was moulded around real human skeletons. When Lelli died, his wife Anna Morandi and an assistant continued the business. His wife, a truly talented woman, believed that to understand a human organ you had to touch and feel it. She immortalized her husband in a statue with his hand touching a human heart. It may seem a little gruesome to us today, but for Anna Morandi in the eighteenth century this was a romantic gesture: she is telling us that her husband was a sensitive, feeling person when it came to matters of the heart.

For the next hundred years, the Bolognese school of wax modelling continued to preserve the afflictions and deformities of the common man. In an age when being diseased meant being an outcast, these figures offered invaluable insights into people whom society normally chose to forget. They are not only medical tools, but portraits of the forgotten.

MANTUA: THE PALAZZO TE

In Lombardy there is a beautiful region of lakes and rivers, where lotus flowers blossom in summer and the waters shine like mirrors in winter. And from these waters rises a magnificent, fairytale city that was once the domain of a great family of princes: the Gonzaga. But there was a time when it wasn't so beautiful. When the Pope came here in 1459 he complained that the town was marshy and malarial. That was an insult that the Gonzaga were not prepared to stomach, and the result was that they called upon Italy's greatest artists to make their city as magnificent as Rome. Leonardo da Vinci, Michelangelo and Titian were all commissioned, but probably the most striking contribution came from an unknown artist who arrived in Mantua in 1524.

When Giulio Romano met the Gonzaga prince Federico they walked about the fields outside the town and the prince told him he would like a little place where he could go to relax; what he actually meant was that he desired a pleasure palace in which he could entertain his mistress. Romano was quite an appropriate choice for this kind of commission, because he had previously been asked to pack up and leave Rome after upsetting the authorities with a series of pornographic engravings that showed in the most graphic detail his sixteen favourite sexual positions.

The Palazzo Te is the resulting 'little place' – and it is distinctly 'aphrodisiacal'. The Hall of Psyche, antechamber to Federico's bedroom, is covered in paintings depicting the sexual antics of characters from classical mythology. Polyphemus is shown as a muscular giant wielding an enormous priapic club, with Federico Gonzaga's name inscribed above him; Cupid and Psyche disport themselves on their marriage bed (Venus, Cupid's mother, had tried to prevent their marriage in the same way that Federico's mother had tried to put a stop to his relationship with his mistress).

But the highlight of the palace is most definitely the Room of the Giants. To stand in this room is like being in the centre of a terrible disaster: the giants have attempted to climb up to heaven to defeat the gods, but Jupiter, father of the gods, has thrown his thunderbolt and sent them crashing back down to earth. All around, great rocks tumble down and smash on to the heads of the giants. It is a masterpiece of perspective, encompassing every wall, and Romano even gave the room the characteristics of an echo chamber to enhance the feeling of enormous space.

As a result of the way he completed Federico's commission the hitherto unknown Romano became hugely famous not just in Italy but far beyond. He was the only artist whom Shakespeare ever praised by name, referring to him as 'that rare Italian master'. Together, Federico Gonzaga and Romano Giulio created a revolution in art. From this period onwards, art was for pleasure.

OPPOSITE: The fantastic *trompe l'oeil* gods of Olympus on the ceiling of the Room of the Giants in Mantua's Palazzo Te.

BELOW: A leering satyr and nymph in the Hall of Psyche.

OVERLEAF: The magical approach to the city of Mantua, where the Mincio river forms three lakes that surround the northern part of the town. Until the eighteenth century, the southern side was also enclosed by marshes, which were then drained.

ABOVE: In addition to all the violin workshops, Cremona is also famous for its *torrone*, a hard kind of nougat.

CREMONA AND THE SOUND OF STRINGS

Roughly halfway between the cities of Mantua and Milan lies the little town of Cremona, which is most famous for its violins. Not only was the violin invented here 500 years ago, but this remains the manufacturing centre. Perhaps the most romantic of all musical instruments, the violin expresses nuances of emotion and passion that no other instrument can hope to reach.

The great violins of Cremona are housed in the Palazzo del Comune, the town hall. They include the oldest and most precious violin in the world, known as the Amati after the inventor of the instrument, Andrea Amati. In 1564 King Charles IX of France heard of this new invention and ordered 38 of them. The instruments that Amati produced for the king have been the model for all violins since, with their scroll neck and their curving shape based, it is said, on the figure of a woman.

The type known as the Stradivarius is still the most famous of all, even if the refinements brought in by Amati's pupil Stradivari seem minimal and the sound made by one of them doesn't seem so very different from that produced by an Amati. Violin-making is a family business: the Amati family excelled at it for 200 years, and Stradivari's achievements would have been impossible without the aid of his sons; the family tradition still holds true in the workshops of Cremona today.

As with most great inventions there is no end to imitations of these historic violins. But the 'goat violin' of Valchiavenna is not something I would recommend to an orchestral player. A variety of cured meat, it owes its name to its shape, which is similar to that of the musical instrument. This gastronomic delight consists of the shoulder and thigh of a goat, with the leg acting as the neck of the instrument and the muscular mass as the case. By tradition, when slicing it you are supposed to handle it like a violin, resting it upon your shoulder and using the knife like a bow. Italians are artists when it comes to food, too!

TOWARDS MILAN

The Visconti family are said to have founded a state 'with the sword and the crucifix'. They were originally from the Lake Maggiore region and they came into prominence through boldness and determination in the Middle Ages in an Italy fragmented into tiny factions constantly at war with one another. It all began on the freezing night of 21 January 1277, when Cardinal Ottone Visconti, with the support of the Roman Curia, defeated the della Torre family, who had been excommunicated for their anticlerical attitudes. In this way the cardinal became Archbishop of Milan and absolute ruler of the richest and most densely populated city in northern Italy.

Of the twelve Visconti who left their mark on Milan, Bernabò, born in the early fourteenth century, was probably the cruellest – a bitterly anticlerical persecutor of the clergy.

During those rare moments when he was not killing or torturing his enemies he would retire to his library to consult Arthurian romances, researching details for the knightly tournaments he liked to organize – and to win. According to some chronicles, when two Benedictine monks, emissaries from Pope Innocent VI, came to the castle of Melegnano to deliver a certificate of excommunication he met them on the drawbridge over the River Lambro, asking them if they preferred to drink or to eat – which was to say, to be drowned or to swallow the Papal Bull. The two men chose to eat the document with its leaden seals, and were then allowed to return to Rome. A papal envoy who entered Milanese territory to publish a proclamation against a friend of Bernabò's came off much worse: he was captured, tied to an iron grille and then slowly roasted to death.

Bernabò's ferocity did not spare even his own (illegitimate) daughter; she was arrested, accused of adultery, tortured and walled up alive in the Rocchetta of Porta Nuova, where she died after months of suffering. Bernabò's tyranny was brought to an end in 1385 by his nephew Gian Galeazzo, who locked his uncle up in the tower of the castle of Trezzo, where he was subsequently poisoned.

ABOVE: The intricately ornamented marble façade of the Certosa di Pavia is one of the masterpieces of Renaissance decorative design.
OPPOSITE: The priest I met here is studying the continual evolution of the building complex, where nearly every architectural style since the fourteenth century is represented.
OVERLEAF: The Galleria Vittorio Emanuele II, still a busy shopping centre, is an early example of the extensive use of steel and glass in building construction.

Milan was where the Visconti and later the Sforza families lived and ruled, but the monastic complex of the Certosa, dedicated to the Madonna delle Grazie, was where they went to die. Known also as the Carthusian Monastery of Pavia, it is one of Italy's most extravagant buildings, built on the initiative of the same Gian Galeazzo Visconti. Work began in 1396, but it took 150 years to complete; the façade alone took 87 years. The Certosa brings together five centuries of Lombard art, from the Gothic to the Baroque, and the intricate craftsmanship is impeccable. Surprisingly for a religious monument, it shows images of pagan Roman and oriental emperors. Gian Galeazzo also had a monastery built behind the church, so that the monks could look after the family burial-ground. Originally it belonged to members of the Carthusian order, whose cells range round the sides of the cloister; it is now run by Cistercians, and you can only see inside with their permission.

A hundred years after it was begun, Visconti's magnificent creation was eventually completed by his great-grandson Ludovico Sforza. Inside the Certosa you will find the funeral monument to Ludovico, with his beautiful wife Beatrice d'Este beside him; she died in childbirth when she was only 21 years old. It is these two, not Gian Galeazzo Visconti and his wife, who dominate the Certosa, and it is they who seem to be honoured by all this beauty.

Nearly five centuries later, when the hotch-potch of small states, most of them foreign-dominated, was welded into a unified Italy, Milan became the location for the first great monument of our new nation. It wasn't a church or a palace, but a shopping arcade near the cathedral. The Galleria Vittorio Emanuele II, named after Italy's first king, was designed in 1865 by Giuseppe Mengoni who worked on it for ten years before being unfortunate enough to fall to his death from the roof only days before the opening ceremony.

This arcade was far more than a precursor of the ubiquitous shopping malls found throughout today's industrialized world. It was a manifesto for a new Italy: a land of wealth, consumerism and miraculous engineering. The floor carries symbols of the various Italian cities: Romulus and Remus for Rome, the fleur-de-lys for Florence, a bull for Turin and a white shield with a red cross for Milan. Over the intervening 150 years the Turin bull has acquired an indentation on his testicles: apparently it brings good luck if you put your heel on the spot and can spin all the way round without overbalancing. The mosaics beneath the roof display the ambitions of the new nation. Beautiful white women, representing Italy, are shown having goods brought to them by black workers from all over the world. It's a little embarrassing today, not very politically correct, but fortunately people are usually too busy looking into the windows of the smart shops to notice. Italy – certainly later, under Mussolini – really did want an empire like Britain and, to a lesser extent, some of the other European nations. Although we never gained much land, and lost fairly rapidly what we did gain, we did get an empire of sorts: a fashion empire, and Milan is its acknowledged centre.

The fabric of Milan was devastated during World War II. Since then buildings have gone up and come down. Everything is in a state of constant change. But at its heart, Milan's most precious treasure manages to survive in the church of Santa Maria delle Grazie: *The Last Supper* by Leonardo da Vinci, the most famous painting in Italy.

Since the 'economic miracle' that took place in Milan in the 1950s, the city has been the powerhouse of Italy. It does not contain our country's soul, like Rome or Naples, but people say it has the brain; this is where the money comes from, where business happens. For me, coming to Milan is like going to New York. These people are not like other Italians, and especially not like us lackadaisical Venetians. Here everyone always has somewhere to go and people to see.

THE LAST SUPPER BY LEONARDO DA VINCI

TIME HAS NOT BEEN KIND: this work of art has only been kept alive through endless cosmetic surgery. Leonardo da Vinci was experimenting with a new form of fresco that didn't really work, so within decades *The Last Supper* began disintegrating on the wall of the convent of Santa Maria delle Grazie on which it had been painted. In the Napoleonic Wars, French troops used the room as a stable; in World War II, a bomb destroyed the whole room except for the wall in question. But even in its decrepit state, like an ageing sovereign, the Last Supper remains masterly. This is one of the jewels of Western civilization. A painting so perfect that right from the moment it was completed it was hailed as a masterpiece.

What is it that makes *The Last Supper* so great? The dramatic and vivid expressions of the disciples. The sense of perspective that seems to place us in the room as well. The attention to detail: the bread rolls, the folds in the tablecloth. Artists had been depicting the Last Supper for centuries. They always showed Christ, having declared that one of the disciples would betray

him, identifying the traitor as Judas. But Leonardo breaks this tradition by showing the moment before the identification of Judas, when Christ says that someone will betray him, but not who. The tension is evident: is it him over there? The one next to me? Or, God forbid, have I done something unknowingly to betray my lord? Yet some people claim this painting is not about friendship and betrayal, but about carnal love. The disciple on Christ's right is not John, but instead could be Mary Magdalene – and the face of 'John' does indeed look feminine. Could Christ have married Mary before his death, and could she have borne his son? But just to contemplate a woman at the Last Supper is blasphemy!

Representations of the Last Supper are still created to this day in a small village in southern Italy where, during the Holy Week rituals, the Apostles are impersonated by members of the religious confraternities. By tradition the role of Judas, the traitor, is played by the poorest member of the community, who gets the consolation of taking home all the food set out on the table for the meal.

Towards the end of the fifteenth century, after the last of the Sforza dynasty, Ludovico il Moro, had commissioned Leonardo to paint *The Last Supper*, he gave him a further task that would draw upon his inventive powers. Knowing that Leonardo was an expert in such matters, he asked him to extend the network of irrigation canals on his lands. The Villa Sforzesca, the country house of Beatrice d'Este, Ludovico's consort, situated in the Parco del Ticino near Milan's Malpensa airport, has a highly complex and efficient water-supply network; Leonardo created it, designing artificial canals, waterways and innovative mills and moderating the flow of water downhill through systems of locks and feeders.

ABOVE: Leonardo da Vinci's *The Last Supper* in the convent of Santa Maria delle Grazie in Milan.

BELOW: The Pirelli Tower is Milan's tallest building and it was constructed in the late 1950s according to a design by Giò Ponti.
OPPOSITE: The Colleoni Chapel in Bergamo was built by a family that made its fortune as mercenaries, especially on behalf of the Venetian Republic. The design is by Giovanni Antonio Amadeo, who also contributed to the façade of the Certosa di Pavia.

But this buzzing city is vital in other ways, too: it is home to two of Italy's most important football teams, AC and Inter, and the stadium of San Siro is considered one of the great temples of the game. Football itself is said to originate from a Roman ball sport practised by legionaries, and the way it is played recalls the battle order of the Roman army. However, Italians had to wait until 1893 for the beautiful game to return to their country, when British immigrants set up the Italian football league. It was also an English man, Alfred Edwards, who founded AC Milan as 'Milan Cricket and Football Club'. It is in his honour that the club has always kept the English spelling of its name, rather than using the Italian 'Milano'. The cricket has long since disappeared altogether!

Perhaps the most telling secret that football reveals about the Italians is that to put one over on somebody marks you as a winner, and to an Italian this is one of the most important things in life. Italians lose wars as if they were games of football, and lose games of football as if they were wars. But in the end, in the words of the writer Ennio Flaiano who collaborated with the director Federico Fellini on *Vitelloni*, *La Dolce Vita* and *8½*: 'The Italian only has one real enemy: the football referee, because he delivers a judgement.'

THE SHOCK OF THE NEW

Lake Como, in the shape of an upside-down Y with its two forks ending respectively in the towns of Como and Lecco and the peninsula of Bellagio in the centre, has appealed to Italian poets and artists for many hundreds of years. Since the nineteenth century it has also attracted numerous famous foreign visitors, from Shelley to Longfellow, Stendhal, Flaubert, Liszt and Mark Twain, the last of whom wrote appreciatively in 1869 in *The Innocents Abroad*:

> *From my window here in Bellaggio* [sic], *I have a view of the other side of the lake now, which is as beautiful as a picture. A scarred and wrinkled precipice rises to a height of eighteen hundred feet; on a tiny bench half way up its vast wall, sits a little snowflake of a church, no bigger than a martin-box, apparently; skirting the base of the cliff are a hundred orange groves and gardens, flecked with glimpses of the white dwellings that are buried in them; in front, three or four gondolas lie idle upon the water – and in the burnished mirror of the lake, mountain, chapel, houses, groves and boats are counterfeited so brightly and so clearly that one scarce knows where the reality leaves off and the reflection begins!*

On the south-western side is Como, where in 1745 a creative man in a different discipline, Alessandro Volta, was born into the Lombard aristocracy. His first studies were in the classics but he soon developed an interest in natural sciences, in particular exploring electrical phenomena, a field that would become his speciality. Since the end of the fifteenth century it had become customary for students to attend several universities in different cities, attracted by the fame of the professors. This was what the Polish-born Renaissance astronomer Nicolas Copernicus had done, studying medicine, mathematics and astronomy before coming to Italy to study law in Bologna and then medicine in Padua, ending up in Ferrara where he graduated in canon law. Volta, by contrast, was more of a self-taught man.

Volta's numerous discoveries, inventions and achievements included the installation of his country's first lightning conductor in 1765. Ten years later his continuing interest in the phenomenon of electricity led him to develop a device called the electrophorus, which was used to generate static electricity. And the bubbles of gas that he had seen rising from the stagnant water in the reedbeds of Lake Maggiore, today known as methane, were used by him in 1777 in a pistol whose firing mechanism was operated by 'inflammable air'.

OPPOSITE: Lake Como lies between the Lugano and the Bergamo Alps, 50 kilometres north of Milan. Narrow and fjord-like, the lake fills the glaciated valley of the River Adda, which flows through it.
BELOW: Part of the gardens of the Isola Bella on Lake Maggiore. The Baroque island paradise with its white peacocks, statuary and grottoes, and layers of terracing planted with palms, oranges, lemons, camellias and magnolias, was created out of a barren outcrop of rock for the Borromeo family in the seventeenth century.

ABOVE: Alessandro Manzoni set his famous novel, *I Promessi Sposi* (The Betrothed), on the shores of Lake Como. First published in 1827, this dramatic tale of two young lovers in a time of war, famine and plague, displays rich characterization and a profound insight into the workings of history and the politics of the time.

In the final years of the eighteenth century there was a long academic dispute with his fellow scientist Luigi Galvani about the source of energy that could move a frog's legs when they were in contact with two different metals. Galvani said that the animal tissue was responsible, but Volta experimented with metals alone and found that an electrical current could be produced in the absence of tissue. The matter was clinched in 1800 when he announced in a letter to the prestigious Royal Society of London the creation of the first electric battery (known then as the Voltaic Pile), which used alternating discs of zinc and iron separated by layers of cloth soaked in salt water to produce a lasting electrical current. In 1801 after demonstrating it to Napoleon, he was rewarded with a high office in the Napoleonic kingdom of Lombardy.

This was not the only recognition of his achievements. In 1774 he had been appointed professor of physics at the Royal School of Como, and five years later became professor of physics at the University of Pavia. Political changes were immaterial. In 1815, after Napoleon's downfall, the Austrian emperor promoted him to director of the philosophical faculty at Pavia. And in 1881, long after his death in 1827, his name was assured of immortality in the volt – the standard unit of electrical potential difference.

Not everyone was convinced of the benefits of his principal invention, however: in 1849 a London doctor, James Murray, published *Electricity as a Cause of Cholera and Other Epidemics*, in which he claimed that every illness was brought about by alterations in the natural level of electricity in the human organism. Having established what he asserted was a normal level, he specified the precise changes that corresponded to particular illnesses: for example, a rise of more than 10 units was responsible for rheumatism, while one of 100 provoked madness; similarly, a drop of 10 units caused influenza and a drop of 90 bubonic plague.

In 1899, to mark the centenary of Volta's invention of the battery, a splendid exhibition was held in his home town, opened by King Umberto I. Unfortunately, 50 days later a fire broke out and rapidly reduced everything to a mass of smoking rubble, twisted, blackened iron and ashes. Ironically, the catastrophe had been caused by a short circuit. But just six weeks later the exhibition was reopened to the public, thanks to a miraculous burst of energy and determination on the part of industrialists and enthusiastic citizens. Giacomo Puccini was invited to write a piece of music for the occasion: he produced a brilliant march for piano entitled 'Scossa Elettrica' – Electric Shock.

ABOVE: The shore of Lake Maggiore, at Stresa, where the Miss Italia competition was revived in 1946, following World War II.
OVERLEAF: The Italian Alps, looking across the corn fields of northern Italy towards the Gran Paradiso National Park.

FROM THE MOUNTAINS TO THE SEA

I had been this way before, coming down from the Alps and then crossing the Apennines. It was when I made my way from Aosta, where I had attended the Alpine Military School for five months, down to Pisa, where the parachuting school was situated. The first station on the train journey south was Turin, once the capital of the Savoy dynasty, which gave Italy its first king 150 years ago. In the mid-eighteenth century King Charles Emanuel of Sardinia, of the same family, had issued 'credit notes towards the Royal Finances of Turin', considered to be the first example of state-produced paper money in circulation in Italy.

But now another powerful family, the Agnelli, rules this domain. Their remarkable rise over the last century is all down to one thing – cars. Italian men are romantic, to be sure, but it's hard to tell which they love best, their women or their cars. While for the rest of the world the love affair has gone sour, Italians still adore cars and driving despite smog and congestion. Within the last half century the number of cars circulating in Italy has grown from just over half a million to over 33 million.

Giovanni Agnelli, who began his career as a cavalry officer, introduced cars to Italy when he set up the Fiat (*Fabbrica Italiana Automobili Torino*) factory here in Turin in 1899. Within 16 years, Fiat grew from a single factory with 50 workers to 10,000 employees and an output of 4000 vehicles a year. The distinctive Lingotto factory, opened in 1923, provided the prestige the company needed: a symbol of the modern world. Remarkably, everything was done in-house: sheet metal would go in one side and a car would roll out the other. The highlight was the test track on the roof of the Lingotto factory, where each model would be trialled and perfected. Rarely has a single company so completely changed the face of a major city. Turin's population today is five times what it was 100 years ago, and that is undoubtedly down to Fiat who built entire suburbs for the hundreds of thousands of immigrant workers. It wasn't that Fiat ruled the city, Fiat *was* the city.

The hills of Piedmont were my companions as the journey continued through Monferrato, where my mother spent part of her childhood during World War II. My grandfather was a prisoner of the Anglo-American Allies while my mother, uncle and grandmother were hemmed in by Nazis and partisans, here among the tranquil vineyards, in a property that had somehow been inherited by my grandmother, although the family was based in Sicily.

This is not only wine country; Alba is the white truffle capital of the world. Truffles are fungi that grow underground near the roots of trees, and are sniffed out by specially trained dogs (or pigs in France). These rare and expensive delicacies, prized by chefs and gourmets and reputed to have aphrodisiac qualities, are aptly known as 'white gold'. One French gourmet has distinguished two kinds of truffle-eater: the one who believes that truffles are good because they are expensive, and the one who knows that they are expensive because they are good.

Once the traveller has crossed the Apennines from west to east, the sea finally appears again: the Ligurian Sea, more intense in its blueness than the Adriatic Sea beyond the Venice lagoon, and more suggestive of freedom. This sea has always fascinated me: I was only eight when I heard that Christ lived under the water off the coast here, which was a strange enough idea to prompt me to learn to dive and see for myself. Off the coast of San Fruttuoso, between Camogli and Portofino, an enormous bronze figure with arms outstretched, stands 18 metres beneath the waves. It is the work of Guido Galletti, from the twentieth century, in memory of all those lost at sea, during peace and war, and of those who have devoted their lives to the sea.

Civilization here began on the mountains but has always looked out to sea; Liguria, protected by the Apennines and by its mild climate, takes its name from the ancient people known as the Liguri, who were already living here at the beginning of the first millennium BC. The capital of this region, the port of Genoa, later became one of the four Marine Republics of Italy, together with Venice, Pisa and Amalfi.

It is a land with two faces: the harsh, seemingly impenetrable landscape of the mountains, and the more 'humanized' landscape along the coast, with its picturesque fishing villages.

The hinterland of Liguria is a craggy landscape of scattered rocks and stunted bushes, twisted olive trees and dry-stone walls; steep, winding tracks lead to isolated, half-forgotten hamlets. The inhabitants have learned how to squeeze a living out of the small patches of land fit for cultivation; these people, who, perhaps understandably, have acquired a reputation for tight-fistedness, have created simple but delicious rustic dishes such as *pesto*, made from basil, cheese, olive oil and pine nuts, and *focacce*, flat cakes of bread enriched with oil, sage, onions or cheese. On the coast the village of Portofino has long been a romantic retreat for the stars and a paradise for the paparazzi: Humphrey Bogart and Lauren Bacall, Richard Burton and Elizabeth Taylor used to visit, and today's most prosperous Italians – notably Silvio Berlusconi, the Dolce & Gabbana duo and the president of Telecom Italia – have holiday villas and keep sailing boats here.

My family too has a house: it stands on the hill of Sant' Ilario, above the resort of Nervi, and overlooks the sea. When I was a boy we would spend the summer here together with my Sicilian grandparents. The house, built in Art Nouveau style for my great-grandparents, was named after my grandmother Delia – I have given the same name to my daughter. I loved diving from the rocks into the sea. But as an Italian male, however young, I couldn't simply dive. I had to wait until there were lots of girls looking – and then dive!

As it happens, the singer-songwriter Fabrizio De André wrote a piece called '*Bocca di Rosa*', a bittersweet tale of life and love that celebrates this little hilltop village. One day a beautiful woman who called herself *Bocca di Rosa* – Rosebud Lips – stepped off a train at the little station. While some make love to escape boredom and others do so purely as a business, she made love out of passion. All the men, from the poorest peasants to the principal citizens, availed themselves of her charms and generosity. But in the end the wives decided they had had enough and demanded that the authorities send Rosebud Lips away. With tears in their eyes the local police, decked out in their best uniforms, escorted her back to the railway station. The village priest insisted on walking beside her in the procession, preceded by a statue of the Virgin Mary – sacred and profane love together. And so the joy and happiness that for a short while Rosebud Lips brought to the village disappeared with her down the railway line.

My own family still loves to spend holidays here, between the sea and the magnificent public parks of Nervi, just beneath the precipitous flights of steps that lead from Sant' Ilario. The children like to feed nuts to the squirrels; they are very familiar with the statue of the 'Lady of the Nuts', perhaps the best-known sculpture in the cemetery of Staglieno. This lady, who made a fortune selling dried fruit, requested that on her death she should be buried in this cemetery, which was popular among the Genoese bourgeoisie in the nineteenth century. The hillside is lined with monumental chapels in Gothic, Byzantine, Egyptian, Art Nouveau, Mesopotamian and neoclassical architectural styles, as well as a small-scale copy of the Roman Pantheon and another of Milan Cathedral. The writer Ernest Hemingway described this place

as 'one of the wonders of the world', while the philosopher Friederich Nietzsche declared: 'I love you, grotto of sepulchres, great marble lie.'

Among its inhabitants is Oscar Wilde's wife Constance, who died at the age of 40 in the little seaside village of Bogliasco, having escaped here from the scandal and outcry aroused by her husband's sexual activities in less liberal times than our own. But her serene exile at the Villa Elvira, amid olive groves overlooking the sea, lasted less than a year; after an accidental fall she died in the hospital of San Martino, far from the talented man with whom she had been so desperately in love, and whom she had described as 'my hero'. Wilde, once released from prison, came to visit her grave and bring flowers. Observing the beauty of the location, he wrote: 'I was deeply affected with a sense … of the uselessness of all regrets.'

It was from this coast that the nineteenth-century patriot Giuseppe Garibaldi set out with his small army on his Sicilian adventure, which was to win the Bourbon Kingdom of the Two Sicilies for Italy and move our country one step closer to its eventual unification. On that occasion he had a sponsor: on 29 April 1860 the Lane Borgosesia company signed a bill of exchange for 501,000 lire made out to the shipowner Rubatino, chartering two sailing ships, *Piemonte* and *Lombardo*, for Garibaldi. Meanwhile, Alessandro Antonini, founder of the company, donated the woollen yarn to make the legendary red shirts worn by the Thousand, as Garibaldi's followers were known. The colour is still known today as 'Garibaldi red'.

ABOVE: Camogli is a charming fishing village where I have often enjoyed listening to the rumbling of the waves breaking on the pebble beach.

OPPOSITE AND OVERLEAF: The village of Portofino is shaped like a crescent moon, wrapped around the bay. The façades of the houses are painted in the colours of the region – soft yellow, rusty red and faded pink. My children love it here.

2

HEADING FOR THE HILLS

MEDIEVAL TOWNS, PALACES & ART

Tuscany – Pisa, Lucca, Florence, San Gimignano & Siena;
Le Marche – Urbino; Umbria – Assisi & Orvieto

ABOVE: Unlike most of the north of Italy, many parts of Tuscany still offer unspoilt and uninterrupted views.
PREVIOUS PAGE LEFT: The hills of southern Tuscany.
PREVIOUS PAGE RIGHT: The Basilica of St Francis of Assisi, framed by the Umbrian countryside. Since I was a young boy I have been impressed by the serenity of the brown-robed Franciscan monks who wander around wearing sandals, even in winter.

When, 20 years ago, wearing military uniform topped with the plumed hat of the Alpine Regiment, I made my way to Pisa near the Tuscan coast for a parachuting course, my imagination was fired by historical events of a generation earlier. I was near the Gothic Line or Green Line, a few dozen kilometres north of the River Arno. A huge defensive position built by German soldiers in 1944, towards the end of World War II, it cut the Italian peninsula in two in order to prevent the Allies reaching the Po plain from the south. In places it was 30 kilometres deep, bristling with minefields, barbed wire, anti-tank ditches, trenches, artillery bunkers and machine gun posts; if the Allies managed to cross this formidable obstacle, Germany would soon fall. In September 1944 the Allies began their attack, breaking through the front line at several points, but heavy losses, lack of reinforcements and bad weather forced them to halt for the winter. When the Anglo-American offensive started the following spring the Gothic Line collapsed, but only after it had accomplished its task of delaying the advance. The casualties were enormous on both sides: about 75,000 German and 65,000 Allied troops were killed, wounded or missing. It was a sobering reflection for a young man engaged in safe peacetime soldiering.

A PLACE OF BEAUTY AND TRAGEDY

My journey from the mountains to the sea also aroused other thoughts. At the beginning of the nineteenth century Mary Shelley, wife of the Romantic poet Percy Bysshe Shelley, recounted in her journal how pleasant the Tyrrhenian coast of Tuscany was, with its numerous little villages and its mild and healthy climate, and how wonderful to be able to step out of the house into the sea. But then, one morning in 1822, a body was found washed up on the beach at Gombo, near Viareggio. The flesh on the arms and face had been eaten away, making the victim unrecognizable. It was only from the clothing and a book of poetry in the jacket pocket that the body was identified as that of Shelley. Just a month short of his thirtieth birthday, he had spent the previous four years in Italy after many years of restless travelling. Only here did he find a land where he could be himself: he was English, but the spirit of Italy ran through his veins, and the year before he drowned, he had written these prophetic words in *Adonais*:

> … My spirit's bark is driven,
> Far from the shore, far from the trembling throng,
> Whose sails were never to the tempest given.

Edward J. Trelawny, sailor, writer and a member of the Pisan circle that included Shelley and Byron, had named the boat that gave rise to the tragedy *Don Juan* in honour of Byron. Shelley then changed the name to that of one of his own works, *Ariel*. Of course, this irritated Byron, who had *Don Juan* painted on the forward mainsail.

Mary Shelley asserted that she had heard that this model of boat had a defect and that it was never seaworthy; she thought it looked ungainly and like a coal barge. Her unease proved correct as when a sudden storm blew up the boat did not simply overturn but sank completely.

In accordance with local health regulations, Byron burnt Shelley's body in a funeral pyre on the beach. The poet's heart was pulled from the fire and kept by Mary Shelley. Trelawny took the ashes and had them buried in the Protestant Cemetery in Rome where he was to be buried himself in 1881, alongside his friend. In the cemetery, beneath the Aurelian Walls, lies a stone in memory of Shelley. It bears the words 'COR CORDIUM', heart of hearts, with three lines from Ariel's song in Shakespeare's play *The Tempest*:

ABOVE: Located between La Spezia and Viareggio, north of Pisa, the mountains of Carrara have provided, and continue to provide, pure white marble for creating sculpted treasures and marvellous buildings.

> Nothing of him that doth fade,
> But doth suffer a sea-change
> Into something rich and strange.

His drowning was not forgotten. In 1969, when the Rolling Stones were recording *Let It Bleed*, a member of the band, another wild spirit, Brian Jones, 27 years old and already the father of three children from three different women, drowned in mysterious circumstances in his own swimming pool. At the great free concert held in memory of Brian in London's Hyde Park, before an audience of half a million, Mick Jagger read out two stanzas from Shelley's *Adonais* before releasing thousands of white butterflies. The poet's words resounded in the air:

> Oh, lift me from the grass, I die! I faint!
> I fail! Let thy love, in kisses rain.

ART AND TRADE

The Tuscan coast descends towards Lazio, the region of which Rome is the capital, past the mouth of the Arno, the port of Livorno and the strait of Piombino. Here it looks towards Elba,

RIGHT: Perched atop a volcanic outcrop, the inhabitants of Pitigliano used the steep cliffs as a natural defence.

where Napoleon was confined in 1814 after his defeat at Leipzig, when he was forced to abdicate. He remained on the island for ten months before escaping and being finally vanquished at Waterloo. Along the coast towards the Argentario peninsula there are numerous fashionable seaside resorts, such as Punta Ala near Grosseto. Originally it was known, charmingly, as Punta Troiaccia (Foul Whore Point), and the island just off it as Troia (Whore). Name changes were made during the 1930s due to the complaints of local people, but a few nearby crags retained their old names, such as I Porcellini (the Piglets).

The irony exhibited by the Tuscans is remarkable. In the 1980s, in the Fosso Reale, a canal that flows through Livorno, three sculptures of heads were found. They were attributed by several distinguished critics to a famous son of this city, the painter and sculptor Amedeo Modigliani, who made his name in the vibrant world of early twentieth-century Paris. He was a contemporary of the Cubists, including Picasso and Braque, but never belonged to their movement. Nor did he follow in the artistic tradition of his Tuscan predecessors, such as Giotto or Michelangelo, who had had a positive vision of man and saw him as being in control of himself and of the world, which he faced in a spirit of serene affirmation. Modigliani was sucked in by the frantic pace of life in those days and, influenced by Toulouse-Lautrec and Cézanne, developed his own unique style. The extraordinary elongated heads and attenuated limbs of his figures, with details pared to the minimum, are the work of a natural sculptor, perhaps more intrigued by experimenting with shape than with colour.

Born in 1884 to a Jewish family, Modigliani had a self-destructive streak and was prone to depression. Art served as a refuge; in it he desperately sought some kind of harmony with the world. However, we can judge how difficult he found this task from his words: 'Life is a boiling magma which no one can handle without burning themselves.' The faces he painted, full of passion and profundity, testify to this. His models said it was like having their souls bared. Yet, feeling he had no right to penetrate into the depths of the personalities of his sitters, he often painted their eyes – 'the windows of the soul' – without pupils. Alcohol, drugs and tuberculosis brought the life of this creative genius, the epitome of the tragic artist, to a premature end in 1920.

And here's where the irony comes in. According to an old story, Modigliani had thrown the heads away either because he was dissatisfied with them or because he was enraged by criticism of them. But the sculptures dragged from the Livorno canal were not his creations. Shortly after the 'discovery', three university students from Livorno claimed that one of them was their work, made with a cheap electric drill. Subsequently, after an appeal had been broadcast on television, the man responsible for the other two heads came forward. He was a Livorno dock worker interested in art, who stated that he had done it as part of an 'aesthetic-artistic operation' to discover 'to what extent people, the critics and the mass media create myths'.

The harbour at Livorno was developed by the powerful Medici family, who between the fifteenth and eighteenth centuries ruled first Florence, then all Tuscany. In 1618 Livorno

OPPOSITE: The church of San Biagio at Montepulciano, south-east of Siena, the work of Antonio da Sangallo the Elder, is a fine example of Tuscan Renaissance architecture.

OPPOSITE: The breathtaking sequence of Romanesque marvels in the Campo dei Miracoli – baptistry, cathedral and belltower.
BELOW: Doing what all the tourists do. I took this photograph of my family 'holding up' the famous leaning tower.

became a free port, a cosmopolitan place that formed the strategic centre of English and Dutch trading in the Mediterranean. For English traders in particular, Tuscany played a key role thanks to its neutrality and independence. Free trade was guaranteed in its main port, giving English merchants an alternative to the monopoly exercised by the Levant Company, a group of London merchants, chartered in 1605, who traded principally with ports in the Eastern Mediterranean.

After the peace of 1604 between Spain and England, which ended some two decades of intermittent hostilities, the Grand Tour became an almost obligatory stage in the education of young British aristocrats. Its aim was to introduce them to the glories of European art and architecture from classical times onwards – as a by-product, it helped to fill many of Britain's stately homes with paintings, sculptures, furniture and antiquities acquired along the way. These cultural voyages of discovery were facilitated by the sailors who transported the young men's heavy and voluminous luggage back by sea, and by the merchants who transferred money by means of letters of exchange. Irrespective of religion, debts or legal problems at home, travellers found no problems in Livorno. Goods could easily be transformed into hard currency or they could serve as guarantees to obtain credit and cash. This major Italian port was, in sum, one of numerous mutually beneficial business ventures initiated by the astute and hard-headed Medici.

PISA: A PLACE OF MIRACLES

As young army conscripts in that jewel of medieval architecture, Pisa, it was straight to the bars to meet girls, as soon as my mates and I had time off! In those days I never paid much attention to the beauties of the Campo dei Miracoli, the Field of Miracles, where cathedral, baptistry and belltower combine to form a Romanesque masterpiece. Yet every year hundreds of thousands of people come to this town just to see the belltower, better known as the Leaning Tower of Pisa. Who can truly say they have seen Italy without a trick photograph of themselves 'supporting' the Leaning Tower to prove it?

But I do have at least one clear memory of the Campo dei Miracoli, from when I was about ten. I ran onto the grass at the side of the cathedral and did somersaults, one after another. When I stopped, all the buildings seemed to be spinning around me, and a couple came up to me exclaiming, 'Bravo, bravo, you're very good!'. They gave me a coin which was the first 'honest' money I ever earned. In this incredible place we all have our own emotions and points of view. When the writer Charles Dickens came here in the nineteenth century he knew the tower only from pictures. After he had seen the real thing, he complained that it was too small.

The tower, begun in 1173, is 60 metres high and at the top it leans more than 4 metres off centre. Needless to say, it was originally intended to be straight, but soft soil around the foundations on the south side caused it to incline almost immediately. When it started to lean, all work was

DANTE: CREATOR OF THE ITALIAN LANGUAGE

WHEN WE SAY that we're in seventh heaven we mean we feel a great joy, almost a sense of beatitude. This expression takes us back to the Ptolemaic conception of the universe, with the celestial region divided up into ten heavens, each one ruled by a planet. Only the first seven of these were accessible to man and the seventh heaven was the greatest state of beatitude granted to him; the eighth was reserved for the blessed, the ninth for the angels and the tenth for God. This is how Dante describes them in *Paradiso*, the third book of the *Divine Comedy*.

Dante was born in the city of Florence in 1265; his mother died when he was still a child. In the *Vita Nuova*, a work that most fully expresses the spirit of the *stil novo* (the new style that idealized the object of the poet's love), he tells us how at the tender age of nine he met and fell in love with an eight-year-old girl named Beatrice. There is no doubt that Beatrice actually existed, but Dante's love for her appears to be an idealization of woman as a mystic link between man and God. One day Beatrice married, but died shortly afterwards: her death, even more than her marriage, caused Dante great sorrow. His love for Beatrice was to remain the central episode in his life and the inspiration for his art, even though he himself married and had four children. He named the last child Beatrice and she became a nun.

He wrote several works in Latin, such as *Monarchia* and *Quaestio de aqua et terra*, in which he refuted the notion, much debated at the time, that water at one point on the surface of the earth could be higher than the land. His *Canzoniere*, a collection of amorous lyrics of an

allegorical-philosophical nature, is one of the most elevated and representative documents of that notable period of spiritual life in Italy that gave birth to the school of the *stil novo*.

His treatise *De vulgari eloquentia*, 'On the Language of the People' (Italian as opposed to Latin), remained unfinished. In this work, which

contains errors owing to the fact that the science of linguistics had not yet been developed, he contemplated the possibility of a vernacular language in which the various dialects of the peninsula would be gathered together and harmonized. His greatest achievement in this connection was to establish the Tuscan dialect, in which his *Divine Comedy* is written, as the basis for the modern Italian language.

After many years of wandering he settled in Ravenna and he died there in 1321 at the age of 56. Dante's fame is bound up with his sacred poem, the *Divine Comedy*, which recounts the poet's mystic journey through hell, purgatory and paradise. The poem portrays man in all his faculties, from the lowest to the highest, with unequalled profundity. Virgil, the symbol of perfect humanity, accompanies the poet in the first two worlds, whilst Beatrice, the symbol of illuminating grace, acts as his guide in paradise.

Dante has inspired authors worldwide. He was known to Chaucer and was read and admired by Milton, but it was the Romantic poets who were most deeply stirred by him. Blake drew a number of illustrations for the *Divine Comedy*; like most of his contemporaries he was clearly more excited by the descriptions of hell, than those of purgatory and paradise. Byron saw Dante as a figure of prophecy and Shelley was the first of a number of major poets to try his hand at translating cantos from the *Divine Comedy*. In America the first full translation was by Longfellow. In the twentieth century, T.S. Eliot's poems probably contain more references to Dante than any other writer. Even if his theology may seem remote to many, we can still be thrilled by Dante's visionary power.

ABOVE: The statue of Dante in Verona. The author, soldier, diplomat and magistrate is now seen as the creator of modern Italian.

stopped. It was only some 10 metres tall then. To continue, they knew, would almost certainly lead to catastrophe. But that's precisely what they did.

I often wonder why the Church authorities and architects took this decision, because surely it would have been more sensible to start again. Maybe quarrels between the Church leaders made it impossible to reach any other decision. Maybe they decided it was fate – that God wanted it to look this way. But I like to think that they observed what had been built so far, and just decided that a leaning tower would look terrific. Over the centuries, the tower became one of the most written about, sketched and then photographed sites in the world. The tilt slowly increased, seemingly defying gravity, but still it did not fall.

Mussolini, our Fascist dictator from the 1920s to 1940s, hated the tower's tilt. He loved straight lines – like those of an army battalion. The tower showed signs of insubordination, so he ordered cement to be poured into the foundations to straighten it. It only made the tower tilt even more. Predictions were that it would collapse some time in the twenty-first century. But an extraordinary geotechnical engineering programme undertaken in the 1990s, involving the selective removal of soil from beneath the foundations, has produced such good results that the tower has been declared stable for another 300 years. The building has become a masterpiece of engineering, a celebration of all that is unusual and unique in the world. But in Italy nobody ever wants to be second-best. The inhabitants of a little village called Massimo Visconti, just west of Milan near Novara, claim that their tower leans even more than the one in Pisa – and, as it dates from the early twelfth century, it is even older.

The rivalry between the inhabitants of Pisa and those of the nearby town of Lucca is more dramatic – the latter have a saying: 'Better a dead person in the house than a Pisan at the door!', to which the Pisans reply: 'May God listen to you!' Following the Genoese victory over Pisa at the battle of Meloria towards the end of the thirteenth century, seven leading families moved from Pisa to Sicily. They included the Vanni, my mother's ancestors. In Sicily the Vanni split up into various lineages: the Marquess of Roccabianca, the Prince of San Vincenzo, the Marquess of San Leonardo and the Duke of Archirafi.

Some have maliciously insinuated that there was a further connection with a certain Vanni Fucci, a man of such violent character that he was nicknamed the Beast. In Dante's *Divine Comedy*, Vanni Fucci, along with other perceived enemies and evil-doers, is placed in *Inferno* – hell. Dante divides his vision of hell into a number of circles, distributing its inhabitants according to the severity of their earthly crimes and sins in the Church's – and his own – eyes. Vanni Fucci is encountered well down in the seventh pit of the eighth circle, condemned as a murderer and thief. Along with two accomplices, also named Vanni, he is said to have committed a sacrilegious theft from the sacristy of San Jacopo in Pistoia Cathedral.

At Dante's request, Virgil agrees to descend to the edge of the seventh pit. Here the damned run in terror with their hands tied behind their backs by snakes; when these unfortunate beings are bitten, they are immediately burnt to cinders. Dante observes the transformation of one of the damned and hears that he is Vanni Fucci from Pistoia, whom he had known when alive. Vexed at being found out, Vanni Fucci 'predicts' to Dante that the White party of the ruling Guelf faction in Florence will be defeated by the Blacks, and that Dante, a White supporter, will be exiled.

The division of cities into two factions, religious, political, ethnic or whatever, is common to many cultures but is particularly heartfelt in Italy. In Pisa there is a competition known as the Gioco del Ponte, the Bridge Game, which is held on the Ponte di Mezzo between the armies of the Tramontana (north wind) and the Mezzogiorno (the south) – the two halves of the city separated by the River Arno. The contest dates back to the eleventh century, and in its original version was so violent that the Medici had to change the rules. Nowadays the opposing factions, divided into two teams of 20, try to force their adversaries to the far side of the bridge by pushing a cart weighing over 7 tonnes and running on specially made tracks 50 metres long,

But there are those who prefer other forms of recreation, perhaps less competitive but equally (un)healthy and just as elaborate. We Italians also like places where we can indulge in the *dolce far niente* – where we can simply relax. We've been going to Montecatini Terme, some 30 kilometres north-west of Pisa for hundreds of years. It might seem a strange choice, because the town has no sparkling beaches or wild nightclubs or great museums. But it is built on a natural underground spring whose waters have been praised for centuries for their healing qualities.

REMEMBERING TUSCANY PAST

For me Tuscany is essentially a large house in the hills, where the kitchen water came from a pump that my father's ancient aunts operated with energetic kindliness whenever I asked for a drink. The place is best evoked in my father's own words, as he recalled one magical summer:

An unbroken line of tables laid with Tuscan simplicity, with multi-coloured garlands of flowers and magnolia and laurel leaves to add a touch of gentility, stretched all the way across the central room of the villa, connecting the two entrance doors on opposite sides of the house; both of them were wide open and looked out on to two small valleys in the countryside near Lucca, with the River Serchio flowing through one of them and a meagre tributary through the other, the countryside a rich green after the August rains. The war [World War II] with all its troubles had ended just a few months earlier and through an unexpected and fortunate chain of circumstances all of the members of the large Neapolitan family that lived in the villa had been spared; they had all come together now, weary and prematurely aged, in the hospitable though ancient building which lay on the highest ridge of a hill. The old Countess Minima del Serto, widow of Count Gustavo, who had died over 20 years before, had been joined by her eight children, four sons and

ABOVE: Tettucio is the oldest spa in Montecatini, 30 kilometres north of Pisa. The water has different therapeutic qualities, depending on which spring it comes from; the one I tried had a strange taste, but maybe one gets used to it during the recommended two weeks' stay.

four daughters, a daughter-in-law, a son-in-law and four grand-children; the grandchildren were few in number compared with the previous generation, but they made up for this disparity with their liveliness. The lanterns hanging from tree to tree in the driveway of the villa gave off a hazy white and red refulgence which did not disturb the throbbing glow of the emerald-green caterpillars stretched on the flower-beds and reviving after the heat of the summer afternoon. The sun had just set behind the low mountains towards Viareggio, which lay on the horizon like a craggy set of teeth, and it had left a ruddy glow behind, which still flared upon the villa and the sloping garden walls on one side of the hill. The young grandchildren were waiting for the moon, sitting on a flight of steps that dropped down steeply through the vineyards, together with two cousins who had come up from Lucca for the evening.

ABOVE: A photograph taken at Monte San Quirico, Lucca, in the early 1950s, showing the predominance of spinster aunts in my father's family. This can partly be explained by the losses caused by World War I.

I had at once noticed Orsetta, whom I remembered three or four years earlier as still a small girl with long plaits and a sweet open face, with just a hint of languid melancholy about it. But the evening was a cheerful one, with its own special magic, and the girl's face was aglow as she smiled and her lively eyes flitted here and there; she chattered brightly and the landscape, slowly fading from sight, took on an extra element of romantic tenderness. At one moment it was a wood still visible on the mountains towards Pisa, and the next it was the chiming Angelus bell of the nearby church that seemed to act as a bridge between us – and then she playfully held onto my arm as she made her way down a few steps. We were drawn swiftly into a tightly woven net, while the other two cousins, just a few paces away, also seemed aware of something magic and pure hovering in the air.

The clouds gradually lost their reddish tinge, while the shadows grew thicker and darker on the nearby hills and the mountains towards Pisa, which seemed to loom higher against the pearly sky. Orsetta, flushed and smiling, reached the bottom of the steps and set off at a run down the slope that led to a large iron gate in the middle of a boundary wall; half-closing one side of the gate, she continued more slowly along the tangled grass of a broad avenue that cut through the tall, dense vines. A little surprised, I set off after her, bounding along to try to catch up, already savouring the pleasure of having her by my side.

I went back in my mind to the long evening walks I used to take as a boy, from the villa's terraced gardens to the orchard in a hollow between two ridges, to feel the freshness of the bracing air on my face or to immerse my feet in the meadow cooled by the first shades of the night. Or those times when I would go out to fetch 'flavours' or herbs for Aunt Elvira, eager to go running through the dark and bring them back as fast as I could just to hear her say, 'How quick you've been.' Except for those times when I would stop near the trough with the big stone face, to search the branches of a citrus tree for some ripe fruit, juicy and sweet.

Orsetta slowed down a little, and I caught up with her almost immediately with a last great bound. We couldn't talk as we would have liked to and, while Orsetta looked at me with her lips parted, I found I not only couldn't speak but didn't want to say what I felt.

She gave a slight smile, like a breeze among the pebbles and we were caught in a web of enchantment again, brimming over with thoughts but unable to express them. Then I said: 'Do you see the fountain at the bottom of the steps? It never stops dripping into the stone basin and keeps the meadows wet even in the hottest hours of the day, like a doting mother.'

I said it softly, in a detached tone, almost as if to play down the tender side of these few words, which were so clearly designed to be protective, but my tone was so affectionate that Orsetta suddenly fell silent, touched more deeply than she had expected. Then she tore a petal from a geranium and put it into her mouth, chewing it with her teeth, which readily produced a gentle smile.

'Are you coming? Right now! Everyone's already sitting down!' A voice hostile to these lost moments spurred us on to rediscover the enchanted life back at the villa. I linked arms with Orsetta and my heart skipped a beat as we scrambled back up the steps, fast enough to prevent anyone from suspecting we had been deliberately delaying our return, yet still floating in our memories – already over before they had even begun.

The five tables, set in a line from one window to the other, were not perfectly aligned and their varying width broke the symmetry, even though the broad garland of flowers and leaves stretching from one end to the other, rising and sinking over the unequal levels, made the tables into a sort of train. In the centre of one side sat our grandmother, flanked by her eldest children and their husbands and wives, and at the end of the furthest table, near the front door, sat the grandchildren, happy in the warm scent from the garden and countryside that wafted in with the evening breeze. It was just a meal together, however exceptional the occasion, a great return to everything that had been, and had not been, 20 years earlier.

LUCCA, LOVE AND DEATH

My own memories of these places, those of a new generation, also involve special feelings and a female cousin … But it's time to go down from the hills to the city – a city where everybody gets about by bicycle. This absence of cars makes me feel a little at home – like being in Venice but without the water. I'm talking about Lucca, where the opera composer Giacomo Puccini was born in 1858.

Puccini had only one story: a beautiful and vulnerable heroine falls desperately in love, then dies. It's a simple story, but Puccini used it over and over again to produce masterpiece after masterpiece, operas such as *Tosca*, *La Bohème* and *Madame Butterfly*, or my favourite, *Turandot*, known to thousands (though perhaps unwittingly) from the aria that has become one of the great football anthems: '*Nessun dorma!*'

Nessun dorma! Nessun dorma! Tu pure, o Principessa, nella tua fredda stanza, guardi le stelle, che tremano d'amore, e di speranza. Ma il mio mistero è chiuso in me, il nome mio nessun saprà! No, no, sulla tua bocca lo dirò, quando la luce splenderà! Ed il mio bacio scioglierà il silenzio, che ti fa mia! Dilegua, o notte! Tramontate, stelle! All'alba vincerò! Vincerò! Vincerò!

Let no one sleep! Let no one sleep! You too, oh princess, in your cold room, are watching the stars, which tremble with love and hope. But my secret lies hidden within me, no one shall know my name! No, no, on your lips I will tell you, when daylight comes! And my kiss shall break the silence that makes you mine! Vanish, night! Fade away, stars! At dawn I shall win! I shall win! I shall win!

Puccini's father was the head organist at Lucca Cathedral, the Duomo. His grandfather, great-grandfather and great-great-grandfather had all occupied the position, and when he was only five the town decided that Giacomo must continue the family tradition and he was put into training. He also sang in the choir of the Duomo, and at the age of 22 he composed his first mass. It seemed that Puccini was all set to fulfill his destiny and become a servant to sacred music; there was nothing to suggest that he was to become the voice of tragic love.

But in Lucca Cathedral lies the sarcophagus of Ilaria del Caretto, the beautiful young bride of the Lord of Lucca at the start of the fifteenth century. He had all the wealth and power he could have wanted, yet he could do nothing to prevent Ilaria from dying in childbirth. He was devastated. The great sculptor Jacopo della Quercia carved her sarcophagus for the Duomo: the delicate, frozen beauty of Ilaria's face is haunting, and at her feet lies a sleeping dog, a symbol of her fidelity in life and beyond. I can't help but imagine the young Puccini looking at her every day of his life and being captivated. Slowly in his mind the single germ of an idea must have grown ever larger and more meaningful; it was maybe on account of this that Puccini, after his very religious upbringing, went on to write such passionate, emotional tragedies. Perhaps it's because in Italy we see religion and love in the same way: our religion is portrayed as love for God, with all the passions and emotions of a love affair.

BELOW: San Michele in Foro, Lucca, combines Romanesque and Gothic styles. It was built during the eleventh and twelfth centuries and the elevated façade was added between the thirteenth and fourteenth centuries as part of an unrealized plan to enlarge the entire church.

ABOVE: A bicycle is the best way of getting around the historic centres of medieval towns like Lucca.

RIGHT: The Villa Torregiani-Colonna, near Lucca, was built in the latter part of the seventeenth century. It is thought that the French landscape designer Le Nôtre had a hand in the design of the gardens, which are animated by elaborate fountains and hidden waterworks.

FLORENCE AND THE MEDICI

I first went to Florence as a boy, and was overwhelmed. Art historians call it the home of the Renaissance. At the time, of course, that word meant nothing to me; all I saw was a town full of the most wonderful treasures. Florence was the first Italian city in a thousand years to equal the splendours of ancient Rome. The centrepiece was the dome of the cathedral of Santa Maria del Fiore, at the time of its construction the largest in the world, recognized as a masterpiece of engineering. It is the brightest gem in a city of many jewels.

When, in 1420, Filippo Brunelleschi was made superintendent of the construction of a dome over the existing church, the dimensions of which had already been defined by the work previously carried out, the required diameter was at the limit of what was possible for a stone-built dome. Faith in such structures had been severely shaken by the collapse of the dome of Hagia Sofia in Constantinople. This made Brunelleschi a pivotal figure in the history of architecture. His works have such force of inventiveness and novelty that Florence, while remaining basically medieval, became the epitome of the Renaissance city, and was taken up by the humanists as the 'ideal' city. Brunelleschi, a 'universal man', was an architect, mathematician, sculptor, painter and inventor, a military, naval and hydraulic engineer, a designer of theatrical spectacles and of musical instruments, and a researcher into perspective and even into the structure of Dante's *Divine Comedy*.

When he was entrusted with the dome project, Brunelleschi first created a scale model that was 2 metres wide and 4 metres high. For the structure of the real dome he had bricks laid in a herringbone pattern to reduce the weight, and instead of the conventional wooden framework he adopted a system of masonry in concentric rings as a self-supporting, expanding form. The dome, distinguished by its imposing size and shape, was created with an innovative double calotte (semicircular dome): the outer one, which is thinner, was designed to protect the internal one from environmental conditions, although both worked together thanks to powerful binding groins. Almost 50 cartloads of lime and more than 5000 bricks were used in the construction of this model, and he employed only the best artists and cabinetmakers of the day to complete it, asking even the eminent sculptor Donatello to contribute to its decoration.

How did the miraculous artistic explosion exemplified by Brunelleschi's dome come about? In the fourteenth century Florence was a small republic surrounded by great empires. Florentines were free men, with no king or duke to rule over them, who worked together – trading and banking – and became rich and powerful. The richest and most powerful of them were the Medici family, who, to demonstrate their greatness to the world, began to turn the city itself into the trophy of their success. The biblical figure of David, the boy who killed the giant Goliath, became the unofficial symbol of Florence.

OPPOSITE: A vertiginous view of the cathedral of Santa Maria del Fiore in Florence. The cathedral complex is remarkable for the uniformity of materials used: white marble from Carrara, green marble from Prato and red marble from Maremma.
ABOVE: Houses along the River Arno jut out beyond its banks to make the most of available space.
OVERLEAF: Florence by night – Brunelleschi's *cupola* of Santa Maria del Fiore can be seen from anywhere in the surrounding hills.

before fighting Goliath as an excuse to depict him naked. The statue was sculpted in the 1460s, and it is remarkable how in the space of six decades the expression of the spirit of Florence had moved from that tiny figure on the Baptistry doors to a coquettish naked boy, hand on hip, lording it over the spoils and riches of his defeated enemies. But even Donatello's David, radical as it was, was subsequently eclipsed.

In 1504, all of Florence was amazed as a giant new statue of David was rolled into the main square. It was a triumphant moment for the artist, a young man in his twenties called Michelangelo. A committee of the greatest artists of the age had decided that it should be placed outside the Palazzo Vecchio, the town hall, as *the* symbol of Florence. Although the original is now in the Accademia museum, the copy that stands outside the Palazzo Vecchio, guarding Florence, is still as powerful as ever. The light dances off David's face as he towers nobly and protectively over the passing crowds. He is immortalized in a moment of concentration, sizing up his enemy, taking aim, ready to put his sling into action; focused, determined, ready to do battle, it is an image that still captures the imagination.

What really shocked people at the time was the sheer size of the statue – nobody had made one so tall for a thousand years. Looking back at the little David on the Baptistry doors of a century earlier, it is clear that art had made extraordinary progress in a relatively short space of time. Florence had made progress too. Michelangelo's David was no longer the little man against the giant – he *was* the giant. With this statue, Florence was telling the world that it had become the greatest of all cities.

No less shocking was the fact that this giant was naked. It was one thing for Donatello to sculpt a naked statue for a private client, but

ICONS OF MALE AND FEMALE BEAUTY

THE GOLDEN AGE of Medici patronage of the arts in order to turn their city into a showpiece began with a competition in 1401 to find the best artist to decorate the doors of the Baptistry. A sculptor called Lorenzo Ghiberti won, with a proposal for panels depicting scenes from the Bible. Their combination of intricate design, human detail and technical difficulty is seen as marking the starting point of the Renaissance: the rebirth of

the great arts. The small panel showing David killing the giant Goliath is the image that came to define the great city of Florence – the Florentines saw themselves as the little man standing up to the tyrannical giants of Rome and Milan.

Another image of David, the one by Donatello now in the Bargello museum, was the first nude sculpture since Roman times, and that insolent little fighter caused a revolution. For a thousand years the Catholic Church had branded nudity as shameful. But Donatello cleverly used a biblical account of David taking off his armour

It would be unfair not to search for the female equivalent. Florence isn't short of contenders, not least in the world-famous collection of the Uffizi Palace, housed in a building designed by Giorgio Vasari. He is best known for his *Lives of the Most Excellent Painters, Sculptors and Architects*.

The Uffizi is a harem of beautiful women; mostly painted by men, they are what the artists desired them to be. Artemisia Gentileschi, one of the few female painters of the seventeenth century, painted one of the pictures I most admire in the collection: a scene from the Apocrypha in which a young woman named Judith beheads Holofernes, a wicked tyrant. Gentileschi painted it not long after she had been raped by her teacher, and it testifies both to her terrible suffering and to her loathing of the wickedness of men.

Botticelli's *The Birth of Venus* was commissioned by the Medici in the 1480s to adorn one of their villas. Vasari tells us that he was the son of a certain Mariano Filipepi, and that the name by which we now know him comes from the nickname given to his brother Giovanni, who was small and fat and therefore known as *Botticella*, or Little Barrel.

The beauty of this painting corresponds to a rather old-fashioned ideal, but I still love it: she is so refined, so delicate – and so sexy. Some experts claim that having the second toe longer than the big toe is an unmistakable sign of a beautiful woman. Botticelli shows Venus rising from the sea in a shell, a symbol of the vulva. She is captured in that gloriously innocent moment before being clothed and blown to shore. A truly compelling figure, a mass of contradictions, she is fragile yet defiant, innocent yet sexual – a woman made for pleasure, but seemingly unaware of it.
So while Michelangelo created the ultimate

image of maleness in his David, Botticelli did the same for femininity. The Uffizi is full of many more fine examples of nudes. In the nineteenth and early twentieth centuries it was the first destination for British travellers who came to the city, giving Florence the reputation of being 'the only Italian city with an English accent'.

Michelangelo's statue was in a public place for all to see. It is first and foremost a celebration of male beauty. There is really very little in Michelangelo's statue to remind us that we are looking at a biblical character. The only way that he can be identified as David is through his weapon, the sling; apart from this detail, he is simply a naked man. There are now copies of this statue all over the world. In Los Angeles, for example, the rock musician Norwood Young has created a 'House of David' and there are 16 snow-white replicas on classical columns in the driveway.

OPPOSITE: These days a reproduction of Michelangelo's enormous statue of David stands outside the Palazzo Vecchio, where the original used to be.
ABOVE LEFT: A detail of Botticelli's masterpiece *The Birth of Venus*; she seems to combine the features of a Greek statue with those of the Madonna.
ABOVE RIGHT: Donatello's bronze statue of David

ABOVE: The Medici family crest on the Fortezza Medicea in Siena. The origins of the crest remain obscure; earlier versions had up to eleven balls in the centre. The version pictured here was adopted by Cosimo de' Medici and remained unchanged for the remainder of the duration of the dynasty.

Behind the elegant façade of this sophisticated place lies the age-old story of power and wealth. By the mid-fifteenth century, under the shrewd leadership of Cosimo de' Medici, the family had already become the unofficial rulers of the city even though Florence wasn't supposed to have any rulers. It was a city of free men against giants, so when Cosimo built a new family palace he was careful not to make it too ostentatious. He didn't want to be accused of behaving like a prince. The Medici Palace, like a fortress in the city, may be free of fancy detail but it leaves no doubts about the family's great power. Inside the building is the Medici chapel. Only family members or close friends were allowed into it, and only in that windowless chamber hidden in the heart of the palace do the Medici reveal their true desires.

The subject of the frescoes in the chapel appears suitably religious: the Journey of the Magi, the three wise men who attended the birth of Christ. But in the execution a different story emerges: one wise man and his entourage. The wise man has been identified as Lorenzo de' Medici, Cosimo's grandson and heir. Behind Lorenzo is Cosimo himself. Next to him is his legitimate son, and leading the horse his bastard son. Behind them is a crowd of powerful nobles and merchants of the day. Many of them remain unidentified, apart from Pope Pius II and a number of other important Medici allies. The landscape in the background is a fantastic representation of the Florentine countryside, with little palaces like Medici villas scattered around. Hunting scenes are depicted: leopards attacking deer or cattle, armed men on horseback, birds of prey in hot pursuit.

It is not a biblical scene, but a statement of power. The Medici appear as undisputed rulers of the republic of Florence, riding off in search of new conquests. By the time the people of Florence realized what was happening, it was too late. It was in 1469, on the death of his father Piero, that Lorenzo de' Medici became the ruler of Florence. His father had been known as *Gottoso*, meaning 'gouty' – the disease afflicted almost all the Medici – and was the son of Cosimo, known as *il Vecchio*, founder of the dynasty. In the same year that Lorenzo assumed power he married Clarice Orsini, of the Roman aristocracy; the celebrations were splendid and public, emphasizing the close relationship between the city and the ruling family. The Medici also managed to combine magnificence with austerity, a policy that won them many supporters even among the working population, whose resources the family could draw on thanks to their dominion over much of Tuscany.

At Lorenzo's wedding, gifts came flooding into the palace from the countryside around Florence and from the other cities of Tuscany. They included 150 calves, 4000 hens and ducks, fish, game and countless barrels of wine, which Lorenzo distributed among the people. Clarice Orsini made her entrance into the palace on horseback, accompanied by a procession of knights.

So that everyone could join in the celebrations, banqueting tables were set up throughout the city as well as in the arcades, the loggia and the courtyard of the palace, the ladies being separated from the men. The diners were entertained with dancing, music and other spectacles. Inside the palace, around Donatello's bronze statue of David, tables were laid with rich cloths, brass bowls and great silver vessels full of water to refresh the glasses, silver salt cellars, forks and knives.

LEFT: Cosimo de' Medici, immortalized by Giambologna in the Piazza della Signoria in Florence. Among Cosimo's many achievements was the creation of the Uffizi Palace – originally intended to house the government and now one of the world's greatest art galleries. He also finished the Pitti Palace as a home for the Medici family and created the magnificent Boboli Gardens.

ABOVE: The Ponte Vecchio crosses the Arno at its widest point. The crossing was first created by the Etruscans and has since weathered many storms. As early traffic consisted primarily of travelling soldiers, it isn't surprising that the first merchants to set up shop on the bridge were blacksmiths, butchers and tanners. Under the Medici dominion, these were replaced with the more savoury goldsmiths and arts shops that are still there today.

Each new course was heralded by trumpet-blasts: the servants bearing the food would all halt and wait for a signal to move forward together so that the food could be set down everywhere at the same time. The dishes included roast and boiled veal, mutton, pork, goat and game together with beans, vegetables, spices and piquant sauces, all accompanied by copious quantities of wine. There followed cornets, marzipan, almonds and pine nuts, pancakes, jellies and all kinds of cakes: nearly 1000 kilos of sweets and confectionery were consumed!

Lorenzo himself was a good cook, in an age when the preparation and presentation of food was regarded in civilized countries as an art form, and Italian pastry cooks especially were universally renowned. In his *Canto de' Cialdonai* Lorenzo explains how to make cornets, still familiar to ice-cream-lovers today: 'Put water and flour into the bowl, when you've whipped them, then throw in sweet white sugar: after mixing them together, taste it with your finger; if it seems good then put the moulds on the fire, heat them well and when you put the mixture into the moulds and hear them fry, hold the irons firmly. When you think they are well done, open the moulds and take out the cornets; it is easy to fold them over when they are hot: place them in a white cloth.'

Not only the incarnation of the city's political and financial power, Lorenzo also reflected its love of art and culture; he was the very ideal of the Renaissance prince. A skilful diplomat, he facilitated a long period of peace for Italy, mediating between the various states.

Lorenzo surrounded himself with creative people: writers, poets, painters, architects and artists, such as Pollaiuolo, Botticelli, Verrocchio and Giuliano da San Gallo, who all found him an intelligent and receptive patron. He earned the attribute of 'the Magnificent' and transformed Florence into a lively centre of humanism. This current of thought placed man, the problems of earthly existence and human values over and above the transcendental values that had prevailed throughout the Middle Ages. A man of letters, he would sing his own lines from the 'Triumph of Bacchus and Ariadne'.

ABOVE: Villa Poggio a Caiano, the greatest of the Medici villas, was built for Lorenzo de Medici following a design by Giuliano de Sangallo. Napoleon's sister also lived here, and this is where she supposedly had an affair with the celebrated violinist Nicolò Paganini.

Quant'è bella giovinezza,	How lovely youth is,
che si fugge tuttavia!	Although so fleeting!
Chi vuol essere lieto, sia:	Let all who wish to be happy be so:
di doman non c'è certezza.	Tomorrow is uncertain.

He enriched the family library, sending the scholars who attended his court in search of precious manuscripts throughout Italy and abroad. One of the intellectuals he befriended was Pico della Mirandola, whose prodigious memory was proverbial; he was said to be able to repeat a long sermon after hearing it just once. Passing from the scholastic philosophy of Padua based on the teachings of Aristotle and Averroes to the Platonic philosophy that had established itself in Florence and spread throughout Italy and Europe, Pico did not consider it necessary to choose between the two but rather looked for ways to reconcile them.

This period of peace and prosperity concluded with the death of *il Magnifico* in 1492, which coincided with the end of humanism and the discovery of America. Although Florence, as an artistic and commercial centre, was to be one of the first cities in Europe to taste the new foods from America, such as potatoes, tomatoes, maize, chocolate and turkey, when Lorenzo died Italian politics lost the one man who would have been able to maintain the political balance. Tensions rose again in 1494 when Charles VIII of France invaded the Italian peninsula and Lorenzo's son, Piero de' Medici, fled the city. Heroic figures did come forward, such as a certain Francesco Ferrucci who led the Florentines against the French king, but there were also traitors such as Maramaldo, at whom Ferrucci shouted: 'Coward, you're killing a dead man!'

The dominion of Charles VIII was short-lived; the city came under a republican government led by Girolamo Savonarola, a Dominican friar who opposed the Medici family and who had accused Lorenzo in the last years of his life of having corrupted the Christian and republican city of Florence with his humanist paganism. But Savonarola's rule was so despotic and cruel that in 1498 he was burned alive for heresy. The Medici then returned, with the backing of Pope Leo X and after him Pope Clement VII, who were themselves members of the family.

The succeeding Medici were on the whole cut from poorer cloth, and never again would their star shine as brightly as it had during the early Renaissance. For a while, at the start of the sixteenth century, the family were exiled. But they managed to return to rule as princes on and off for over 200 years, still great patrons of art and culture, even though the artists themselves were not always docile and malleable. Franciabigio, a portrait painter, was a case in point; in his works he accentuated the Renaissance fullness of the figures and the complexity of the compositional schemes, with forms emerging obliquely from shady backgrounds, their faces peering forwards in light that reveals not only their features but also their psychological tension. When he heard that his fresco, *The Wedding of the Virgin*, in the cloister of the church of the Santissima Annunziata, had been admired by the friars before it was finished, he reacted angrily: snatching up a hammer, he smashed it into the head of the Madonna that he himself had painted.

Finally, in the first few decades of the eighteenth century the Medici vanished with Gian Gastone, the last Grand Duke, who showed just how low the family had sunk. He was so lazy that he spent the last years of his life in bed, without ever washing. To clean his mouth while eating, he used the curls of his wig. What an end to such a glorious inheritance!

A SOCIALIST DREAM

In the centre of Italy there is a magical region, a land that takes in parts of Tuscany, Umbria and Le Marche, a land so filled with artistic treasures and natural beauty that it has become the envy of the world. It was here that the Dark Ages were brought to an end, that the forces of tyranny and superstition were challenged and the love of reason, beauty and justice was reborn. And from its lead, the rest of Europe followed. It is a place where people came to learn how to write, how to paint and sculpt, how to cultivate the land and to garden, how to eat and drink, how to behave, how to govern and how to love.

It may seem a sort of fairyland, not part of Italy at all and it has even been given an English-sounding name: Chiantishire. This is a land of picture-postcard views, full of architectural and artistic gems. And sometimes when only ruins remained, British visitors have come along to remake them in their own fanciful style.

In Settignano, not far from Florence, there is a fake romantic castle called Vincigliata. In 1885 John Temple Leader, who had dreams of restoring some ancient feudal pile, bought the ruins of a medieval castle here and rebuilt it in the style of the Gothic Revival. He remodelled the surrounding land as well, planting the slopes with cypresses, pines and ilex trees. He even had medallions struck bearing the words 'Johannes Temple Leader Vincigliatae Dominus', and on the crenellated walls he placed a series of plaques recording the visits to Vincigliata of royal personages, from King Umberto I of Italy to Queen Victoria of England.

But he was only one of many foreigners who have fallen in love with this region and made it their home. In the Val d'Orcia there is a vast estate named La Foce. In the fifteenth century, it was a battleground for warring factions, and the land never recovered until the arrival of an English woman, Iris Cutting, and her fiancé, Antonio Origo. She bought it in 1922, when the land was barren and the inhabitants were living in squalor. But the couple shared a dream of turning more than 30 square kilometres, consisting of 57 farms, into a fertile and thriving community. In a series of much-loved books, Iris Origo recorded her experiences.

At the outset, life must have been very hard and the responsibility she took on was awesome. While Antonio cultivated the soil, working hard to convert this difficult terrain into arable land and building a zig-zag access road, Iris set up schools, a hospital and an orphanage.

It was a socialist dream, to create a 'commune' where everybody worked happily side by side. They managed to survive World War II, having had to evacuate the property when it was taken over

ABOVE: It is impossible for me to think of Tuscany without thinking of their fabulous wines. When I visited the Ricasoli vineyard they lost no time in setting me to work!

by the Nazis, and afterwards they were able to return. Ironically enough the dream ended in the 1960s, with the rise of the Communist movement and increased politicization of the workers. Suddenly the Origos became enemies of the people, and nobody wanted anything to do with them any more.

The centrepiece of La Foce consists of the house itself, built 500 years ago as a pilgrims' hostel on the road to Rome, and the garden, designed by the English architect Cecil Pinsent in the 1920s. It is neither an Italian garden nor an English one, but takes elements from both and also invents a great deal. The idea was to create a garden that would contrast well with the landscape around. And on a hill there is a cemetery that Cecil Pinsent built for the older Origo son, who died when he was nine; here too both Iris and Antonio were buried, as were some of the workers and soldiers who died during the war.

OPPOSITE: Vineyards and olive groves near San Gimignano.
ABOVE: The autumn *vendemmia* (grape harvest) in the Chianti region.

SYMBOLS OF POWER AND RIVALRY

Among the Tuscan hills many castles remain, testifying to an age when power had to be expressed in stone, symbolizing control over the countryside, its trackways and the trade that travelled along them. Each castle has its own history and legends, which together become parallel realities.

On a hill close to Poggibonsi, between Florence and Siena, stands the castle of Strozzavolpe, a square building dating back to the twelfth century. The name – it translates as 'Fox-Strangler' – seems to derive from a legendary fox of violent disposition, which somehow held up the building of the fortress of the Marchese Bonifazio, Duke of Tuscany, and made even the bravest knights flee. A fox-hunt was arranged, but nobody could catch the beast: he would suddenly appear, spitting flames from his mouth, and then go into hiding. Tired of this situation and determined to build his castle, the Marchese decided to be as cunning as his adversary: he concealed himself in the woods, caught the animal in a trap and then strangled it with a noose. The court astrologer predicted that the castle would stand as long as the body of the accursed animal was preserved. And so the Marchese had it embalmed, filling it with a great quantity of molten gold and hiding it in the walls of the castle.

When the moon is full the spectre of the infernal fox is said to wander around the battlements and the age-old trees outside. But it is not the only ghost to haunt the building. A certain Cassandra Franceschi was found with her page-boy in compromising circumstances in the Red Chamber by her husband Giannozzo da Capparello. The husband had them both walled up alive, and ever since their sighs and groans have been heard in various parts of the castle, particularly in the Red Chamber itself.

Tuscany today may seem like paradise, especially to visitors, but it wasn't always so. In the Middle Ages it was an extended battleground where rival towns clashed in the ruthless pursuit of land and wealth. Towns were fortresses first and foremost, and were built on hilltops, with mighty walls and towers, for defence.

The most spectacular hilltop town remaining today is San Gimignano, known, because of its towers, as the Manhattan of Tuscany. But it is nothing compared to what it once was. In the thirteenth century there were 72 towers; now only 15 remain. Unusually, these towers were built to protect the inhabitants not from neighbouring towns, but from each other. The great families of San Gimignano had become rich through trade; they were fierce business competitors who sometimes resorted to fighting in the streets (or from their towers). But the towers were also status symbols – and a town of towers is a sad thing, a town at war with itself, with no sense of civic pride, a place where everything is for the individual.

In an attempt to stop this rivalry, which threatened to banish the sun from San Gimignano for good, the town council decreed that no tower could exceed 51 metres in height. But this didn't stop the great Salvucci family who built not just one enormous tower, but an identical tower next to it.

OPPOSITE: The skyline of San Gimignano. The proportions remind me of New York, even if the dimensions are different.

Towers are at once beautiful and terrifying; San Gimignano destroyed itself with hatred. In the Middle Ages it must have seemed like a vision of hell, with the streets swathed in shadow and hatred rife amongst the citizens. Dante came to the town in 1300, and I can't help thinking that his description of *Inferno* in the *Divine Comedy* is based on this city.

> This fen, which a prodigious stench exhales,
> Encompasses about the city dolent,
> Where now we cannot enter without anger.
> … mine eye had altogether drawn me
> Tow'rds the high tower with the red-flaming summit,
> Where in a moment saw I swift uprisen
> The three infernal Furies stained with blood …

Aggression, internecine as well as against other towns, eventually brought down the wrath of the Florentines, who managed to subdue the place. Plague finished the job, drastically reducing the population and ruining the economy. By the sixteenth century, most of San Gimignano's towers had fallen down – the Florentine authorities had not felt the need to demolish them, for the power these structures had represented had been destroyed: how are the mighty fallen! Only modern tourism has plucked this amazing small town from its subsequent centuries of poverty.

SIENA: EMBODIMENT OF CIVIC PRIDE

If San Gimignano was urban hell, Siena was heaven on earth. In the thirteenth century the city was ruled by the Council of Nine, an elected body that changed every two months. This arrangement made corruption almost impossible, and the system of government brought peace and prosperity to Siena. The Council provided health care and education, commissioned great art works and looked after the poor; and in return the citizens offered undying loyalty. But I think the real secret to Siena's success lies in the design of the city, which was remodelled under the aegis of the Council of Nine.

Its medieval fortified towers, which were like those in San Gimignano, were demolished. Personal coats-of-arms were banned from public buildings. Everybody was asked to identify not with their family, but with their neighbourhood. To encourage this philosophy Siena was divided into *contrade*, neighbourhoods with their own church and flag. When walking in Siena, you feel as if you are being led towards wider streets. And the wider streets lead into even wider streets. And then the main streets bring you down and down towards the centre, to the great Campo of Siena: an amphitheatre where the stage backdrop is formed by the great town hall. By building a new square around the town hall, rather than, as was traditional, the cathedral, the Council was saying that the most important thing in Siena was not God but the city itself. Siena was redesigned with the idea

OPPOSITE: Piazza della Cisterna in San Gimignano, named after the well, with the Torre Grossa in the background.

95

that each citizen would be constantly reminded that he was just one small part of a greater whole.

Siena's unique form of government survived for over 700 years. In the building where the Council of Nine used to meet, the walls bear images reminding councillors how they should behave. The beautifully executed frescoes commissioned from Ambrogio Lorenzetti in 1338, *Allegories of Good and Bad Government*, are masterpieces of medieval Italian art. They also shed light on daily Sienese life, depicting in one half a city governed wisely and effectively, a clean and orderly place embellished with visual delights such as the cathedral and clocktower. (This tower, which can be seen from all parts of the city, is known in Siena as the Torre del Mangia, because in the mid-fourteenth century, just after it was built, the hours were rung by a certain Giovanni di Duccio, known as *Il Mangiaguadagno* or 'Wage-Eater', who had to climb 400 steps to perform his task.) The frescoes showing the city run by a bad government depict crumbling buildings, dirty streets, gangs of thugs and scenes where nobody is working at all, as in Colle Mala Merenda (the Hill of Bad Meals) near Siena, which is said to owe its name to an event that took place in 1337. During festivities organized to celebrate the reconciliation of two rival houses, the Salimbeni and the Tolomei, too few thrushes were brought to the banqueting table and the old grudges resurfaced. Some 20 people died in the subsequent brawl.

Siena's golden age was brought to a tragic end in the late fifteenth century when a great plague killed two-thirds of the population. Since then, the place has hardly changed in many respects: the medieval *contrade* are still the focus of everyday life, and the city relives its history annually with the Palio. This is not just a horse race – it is the life, the soul, indeed the very madness of the city and its people. Passion, life and death, love and hate, the sacred and the profane, kisses, tears and sometimes fisticuffs figure on the day the Palio is run. Although one of the city's gates bears the words '*Cor tibi magia Sena pandit*' (Siena opens its heart even wider to you), this feast belongs entirely to the Sienese; the rest of the world barely exists on this day. There are 17 *contrade*, but after the preliminary heats only 10 of them race. The horse, drawn by lot four days before the race, is the real protagonist, ridden by a jockey known as the 'assassin'. At the end of the race jockeys are often punished if they have lost or been bribed. They ride bareback holding a bullwhip, which they use either on the horse or on their rivals or both. They race just three times round the square, lasting about 90 seconds in all, and then the winning *contrada* can celebrate for the rest of the year.

OPPOSITE: A view of Siena from the tower of the Palazzo Pubblico.
ABOVE: Construction of the Palazzo Pubblico, as the seat of the govenment, was begun in the late thirteenth century.

RIGHT: Siena Cathedral was consecrated in 1179 by the Sienese pope Alexander III, but building and decoration-work continued for more than two centuries. It is one of the finest examples of the Romanesque-Gothic style in all Italy.

OPPOSITE: The *sbandieratori*, skilful jousters, maintain a medieval tradition that dates back to flag throwing during battles to send signals between groups of soldiers. Each flag is made from fine silk and is decorated with the emblem of the *contrada*.

This is not the only Palio in Italy; and some places use not horses but donkeys, recalling the fact that up until World War II many small villages could only be reached by muletracks. In those days donkeys and mules were still the sole means of transport, apart from the villagers' own legs. The donkey races enable these animals to have the best of it for a day over their superior equine cousins; just for once they are something other than symbols of ignorance or stubbornness, and can actually compete in trials of speed and skill. In some towns and villages the winner of the donkey race has to ride to the top of the church belltower. Every winner celebrates with his own *contrada* and kisses his own animal.

THE COURTLINESS OF URBINO

Le Marche was once a forgotten mountainous region on the Adriatic coastline, squeezed in between the great 'empires' of Venice, Florence and Rome. Then, as if from nowhere and in the space of just a few years, it gave rise to one of the greatest courts in all Italy.

OVERLEAF: The rolling landscape of Le Marche brings to mind the paintings of Raphael, who was brought up in the court of Urbino. What we see here has barely changed in hundreds of years.

Travelling towards Urbino, you see it high on its hill like something from a fairytale. In the fifteenth century it was regarded as the perfect city, an inspiration to the rest of Italy and a model for Elizabeth I's court 100 years later in England. It was all the work of one man, Federico da Montefeltro, who came to power purely by chance as the illegitimate brother of the Count of Urbino. When the count was assassinated in a palace conspiracy provoked by his riotous behaviour the town turned in desperation to Federico, who became Lord of Urbino in 1444 at the age of 22. He went on to govern the city and its lands without a break until his death in 1482. Federico was a scholar, a warrior and a man of the people. He was everything that people have expected from a leader since the birth of civilization – although few have lived up to these expectations.

Federico has been depicted as always acting in accordance with the heraldic virtues of loyalty and magnanimity, but there is no doubt that in order to strengthen his own state he also exercised the enlightened self-interest that would be described a little later in Niccolò Macchiavelli's pragmatic treatise on government, *The Prince*: 'Everyone realises how praiseworthy it is for a prince to honour his word and to be straightforward rather than crafty in his dealings; nonetheless contemporary experience shows that princes who have achieved great things have been those who have given their word lightly, who have known how to trick men with their cunning, and who, in the end, have overcome those abiding by honest principles.'

An astute diplomat, both prudent and cunning, when faced with a dilemma Federico would first assess the possible consequences of every option and then take the path that offered the greatest advantages, taking care not to burn his bridges behind him. Federico commanded the best army in Italy and, for the right price, would hire out his services. Soon everyone was indebted to him – except his victims of course. There were moments when he found himself contemporaneously commander of the military forces of the King of Naples, of the Duke of Milan and of the Pope. The Pope promoted him to a dukedom, and even the King of England decorated him. With the money Federico made as a mercenary, he created his great palace.

The first thing to notice as a visitor is a courtyard that is perfect in its simplicity. Federico's virtues are written on the wall here. He is a man of vigilance, of dignity and of martial prowess; but also a man of peace.

Federico opened his palace to some of the greatest figures of the day. He built a vast library to attract scholars and commissioned new buildings for artists to decorate. He summoned the great Piero della Francesca, whose portrait of the duke is one of the most famous of all time. Attributed to the school of Piero della Francesca and conserved in the Ducal Palace of Urbino, the painting *The Ideal City* represents the principles of Renaissance classicism; strictly following the laws of perspective, straight roads are shown intersecting at right-angles, with a monumental building placed right in the centre of the painting.

And it was in Urbino that the great diplomat Baldesar Castiglione set *Il Cortegiano* (*The Book of the Courtier*), constructed as a dialogue between the duchess and the Urbino nobles. A guide to

LEFT: The wonderful orderly courtyard in Federico's palace at Urbino.
ABOVE: Federico's *studiolo* (study) is decorated with intricate and beautiful marquetry based on drawings by Sandro Botticelli.

being the perfect courtier, it became the essential manual for use in courts all over Europe: no self-respecting English knight was ever without a copy. But Castiglione's model proved a hard act to follow. First, the perfect courtier must be born an aristocrat. If your father steers a gondola, or is even a lawyer or physician, forget it. The courtier must be handsome, furthermore. He must be able to sing in tune, to paint beautifully and to write poetry. He has to speak a number of languages and to dance and fence. As a lover, he must be gentle and devoted. He must be patient and determined in order to win his lady's favour through noble deeds, rather than through the force of his character. In behaviour, the courtier must at all times be graceful, eloquent and generous. He mustn't boast or bitch or gossip or flatter. And if he is feeling tired or depressed or grumpy he must conceal his mood so as not to upset the refined aura of the court.

ABOVE: Nuns walking up one of Assisi's steep roads on their way back to the convent.

Castiglione is also very specific about the courtier's apparel. He mustn't be overdressed, like the French, or underdressed, like the Germans, but clothed in a sober and restrained manner. Black is the best colour. As for war, the courtier must be a superb soldier, performing excellently in battle – especially when his prince is watching.

With such high standards, no wonder Urbino's golden age was so short-lived. Castiglione was writing as an old man, long after his fellow-courtiers had passed on, and he was commemorating a bygone age: 'When the windows on the side of the palace that faces the lofty peak of Mount Catria had been opened, they saw that dawn had already come to the east with the beauty and colour of a rose and all the stars had been scattered. From there, there seemed to come a delicate breeze, filling the air with biting cold, and among the murmuring woods on nearby hills wakening the birds into joyous song. Then all, having taken their respectful leave of the Duchess, went to their rooms.'

ASSISI: A PLACE OF GENTLE SAINTLINESS

Umbria, lying landlocked between Tuscany and Le Marche, is another beautiful region of Italy. We think of it as a mystical land, not only because of the strange haze that seems to hang over the landscape but because it has a kind of holiness: Umbria has produced more saints than anywhere else in the world. Like most Italians, I am named after a saint. Although not particularly devout, I can't help associating myself a little with St Francis of Assisi. His 'otherness' was perhaps first displayed when, talking to some village people, he noticed some birds on the ground. To the wonder of the villagers the young man began to converse with these birds, encouraging them to love one another and all God's creatures. It is this gentleness in his nature that has won Francis more followers than those of any other saint.

The saint's father was a rich merchant who called his son, born in Assisi in 1181, Francesco, or 'little Frenchman', in honour of the boy's Provençal mother. As a young man Francis was a rich kid, a playboy, and indulged in wine and women – and this is a part of him that I readily understand. But then something changed when Francis began talking to beggars and lepers, and he stole from

his father to give to the needy. After his crime was discovered he ran away but after a month of living rough, he decided to face his fate. Francis walked back into the place where he had spent his gilded youth – dirty, tired and unshaven. People he had known all his life insulted him, old friends threw dirt and stones at him – but Francis calmly accepted this humiliation.

The bishop summoned Francis and his father to his palace and ordered the young man to return his father's money, to which he immediately agreed. Afterwards he returned stark naked to the crowded courtyard of the bishop's palace. In front of them all Francis declared: 'Please listen, everyone. Because I want to serve God from now on, I am giving my father back the money he is so distressed about and also my clothes … In future I will only acknowledge our Father who is in heaven.'

ABOVE: From the road that winds through the hills towards Assisi, the monumental arcaded walls of the Sacred Convent, with the Basilica of St Francis looming up behind, are clearly visible. The remains of the saint are kept in the lower church and crypt.

ORVIETO: THE OTHER SIDE OF CATHOLICISM

THE GREAT FILM DIRECTOR Federico Fellini once said, 'I am a prisoner of 2000 years of the Catholic Church. All Italians are.' It's difficult to explain to non-Italians the role that Catholicism plays in our lives. As a boy, I felt a spell being cast over me when I came to great churches like the thirteenth-century Gothic cathedral of Orvieto.

For the Capella Nuova in this cathedral, at the turn of the sixteenth century an artist called Luca Signorelli was given one of the most difficult tasks imaginable: to paint, in detail, the unpaintable – the end of the world. Signorelli follows the event as described in the Book of Revelation: first, the world is seduced by the

preachings of the Anti-Christ who, supported by the devil, is addressing a crowd. To one side, the good friars who have opposed his rise are strangled by brutal henchmen. As the Anti-Christ strengthens his hold, there is a scene that eerily anticipates twentieth-century dictatorships – black-clad guards search for dissenters and drag them away for execution. Fortunately, when the Anti-Christ tries to ascend to heaven, as Christ had done, he is shot by an angel, who also destroys his followers in rays of blood.

But it is only a temporary respite, because the end of the world then begins in earnest. Prophets foretell calamity, society falls to pieces and violence breaks out. And then the reckoning begins. Strange angels hunt down the last clusters of humanity like frightened cattle. They fire death rays like flame throwers that incinerate their victims. The world is over, and

for a while there is silence. Then a trumpet sounds and angels summon mankind for the Last Judgement. Naked and bemused, men and women rise from the ground to contemplate a new life. They look around, trying to adjust to this strange place and huddle together.

But it does not last. They are divided into two: the good are sent to heaven, whereas the rest … A terrified man is hoping to escape his fate, trying to get back into the world, but a devil seizes him and beats him. The wicked are carried down all the way down to hell: and there begins an orgy of suffering! Whether you grow up a believer or not, the memory of that image will always stay with you. The frescoes at Orvieto represent the dark side of Catholicism – a fearful warning to sinners, in stark contrast to the kind, gentle, almost paternalistic love shown to his fellow-men by St Francis.

From this time onwards Francis lived in poverty, preaching and healing the sick. He adopted what would become the famous Franciscan habit of rough brown cloth girdled with a simple length of rope. People flocked after him; his message of poverty and sacrifice was contrary to everything that the Catholic Church had become. So when he died in 1226, on the mud floor of a hut outside Assisi, the Pope made a very clever move: he claimed him for the Church. Francis didn't like hierarchy so he had never become a priest, but within two years of his death he was made a saint and the Pope in person laid the foundation stone of an enormous basilica for his tomb. No expense was spared. The greatest artists were called in to paint the walls with lavish frescoes showing scenes from Francis' life.

The crypt where his tomb rests is very moving. The atmosphere, the lighting and the setting have a great sense of theatre that seems almost magical. Four million people visit the basilica every year, a testament to people's love for Francis. But it's difficult not to believe he would have disapproved; his message was one of frugal simplicity – the opposite of what we see in this great basilica. I still think the best place to understand St Francis is in the Umbrian countryside, in the midst of nature, where he was inspired.

ABOVE: The richly decorated façade of Orvieto Cathedral, which is not to be confused with that of Siena. OPPOSITE: One of Signorelli's murals in the cathedral's Capella Nuova, or Chapel of San Brizio, depicting the end of the world.

3

TOURING THE HEARTLAND

ANCIENT DYNASTIES & LA DOLCE VITA

Lazio – Rome; Basilicata – Matera; Puglia – Lecce

ABOVE: The figure of Castor stands next to Pollux, his twin, at the top of the Cordonata, the broad steps leading up to Michelangelo's Piazza del Campidoglio.
OPPOSITE: The interior and exterior of the Coliseum. The name derives from a Roman word for gigantic.
PREVIOUS PAGE LEFT: Rural Italian vernacular architecture – the dwellings of Puglia are known as *trulli*.
PREVIOUS PAGE RIGHT: The Bocca della Verità in the portico of Santa Maria in Cosmedin, Rome.

Italy's capital city, Rome, lies in the middle of the Italian peninsula as you travel north to south, not far from the Tyrrhenian coast. The ancient Roman Empire expanded over a period of 11 centuries, imposing its rule over vast tracts of Europe, western Asia and North Africa. The city itself is said to have been founded on 21 April 753 BC, which just happens to be my own birthday (not to mention that of Queen Elizabeth II, and of course many other people). But leaving questions of legend and astrology aside, what is certain is that Rome was originally a small settlement, built on seven hills, whose citizens managed within a relatively short space of time to conquer all the known world, even though it was surrounded by other powerful peoples such as the Etruscans and the Gauls, the Greeks of Magna Graecia and the Carthaginians.

Thousands of kilometres east lay another highly developed empire, China, whose rulers had decided to seal it from the world beyond by means of the Great Wall. Between this monumental construction and the outlying frontiers of the Roman Empire, defended by the *limes* (fortified lines), lived the 'barbarians', nomadic peoples such as the Visigoths, Ostrogoths, Vandals, Lombards, Avars, Huns, Mongolians and Scythians. In search of new lands, they continually spilled over into the two empires. The regions close to the Tyrrhenian Sea, including Lake Bolsena, were trampled over by invading peoples both before and after the time of the Roman Empire.

The countryside of the present-day region of Lazio, of which Rome is the capital, is still dominated by the aqueducts of the ancient Romans, impressive stone testimonials to a far-reaching system of rule that managed to impose itself thanks to its organization and inventiveness. It was under the Romans, for instance, that a single system for units of measurement was universally accepted. The power of the Empire was based on such practical devices, as well as on its communication routes and engineering skills. The Romans' building methods were so sophisticated that constructions like the Bridge of Nona, built over two millennia ago at the ninth mile of the Via Prenestina, 70 metres long and 15 metres high, are still standing. The Romans were also perfectly familiar with anti-seismic construction techniques; in Rome the Pantheon and the Coliseum are perfect examples, having resisted 2000 years of intermittent earthquakes. Modern science has had to admit that even reinforced concrete, due to its rigidity, is much more destructible in these conditions than the stone, wood and bricks used by the Romans.

Not only that, but the Coliseum was also innovative from the points of view of functionality, versatility and technique. For example, the spectators that flocked to the open-air shows staged here were protected from the sun by an enormous retractable segmented cloth that could be stretched out over the stands when needed. This operation was handled by an expert team of 100 sailors who, for the duration of these events, were stationed at barracks near the amphitheatre, having come up from the port of Misenum. In a cove of volcanic origin in the Bay of Naples, Misenum had been used by the Greeks as a naval base and took its name from Aeneas' trumpeter, who had drowned in these waters. It was in use until at

OPPOSITE LEFT: The shores of Lake Bolsena.
OPPOSITE RIGHT: An Etruscan bronze female figure from the early fifth century BC, used as a dedication at a sanctuary.

least the third century BC, when the Carthaginian Hannibal laid waste to it. A new impulse was supplied when luxury villas were built round about. In the days of the Emperor Augustus (63 BC–AD 14) it became the most important port in the Tyrrhenian, headquarters of the military fleet. It was apparently from here that Pliny the Younger saw the eruption of Vesuvius in AD 79; his uncle Pliny the Elder, who had set out to watch the phenomenon from close up and to help some friends who lived on the slopes of the volcano, lost his life. The older Pliny was the author of the *Naturalis Historia*, a 37-volume work that brought together all the scientific knowledge of antiquity, and was a great observer of the natural world. He suggested, among other things, that the reason geese flew in V-shaped flocks was in order to cleave the air more efficiently. He also noted the behaviour of animals in captivity, reporting that the Romans trained elephants to dance to the sound of cymbals and even to balance on robust tightropes.

Which brings us back to the Coliseum, the temple of spectacles. It was equipped with a series of 28 elevator cages, which went all the way down to stables and stalls 40 metres underground. A system of winch mechanisms, operated by slaves, enabled the captive wild animals to be lifted up to ground level where they would face their human opponents. On a vaster scale, though perhaps less bloodthirsty, were the mock naval engagements staged here. Such grandiose performances with ships were particularly popular; the Emperor Caligula, in order to celebrate the goddess Diana on Lake Nemi, near Rome, had two gigantic ships built just for that purpose. It was the Romans' advanced knowledge of the way liquid behaved that enabled them to transform the arena into a lake. Nor was their awareness of fluid mechanics restricted to entertainment use. It is said that they realized something strange was happening before the destruction of Pompeii because the water began to run faster in the aqueducts.

The Romans' understanding of the physical world was turned to everyday use, too. Ever since ancient times, man had marked out the year basing his observations on the cycles of the sun that marked the progress of the seasons; and so the Latin word *annus*, meaning 'year', was connected with *anellum*, 'ring', signifying the circular trajectory that the sun supposedly travelled around the earth.

The Romans' first calendar contained only 355 days. Since it was different from the solar year, in order to synchronize it with the cycle of seasons an extra month of 22 days was added every so often. Deciding when to do so was a delicate operation and sometimes led to errors. It was Julius Caesar, who ruled the Empire in one capacity or another from 60 BC to his murder in 44 BC, who had this calendar discontinued when it had become almost 100 days ahead of the solar calendar. The Egyptian astronomer Sosigenes was entrusted in 46 BC with the task of establishing the new 'Julian' calendar. It took January, August and December up to 31 days and April, June, September and November up to 30; the year thus amounted to 365 days, with an extra one being added every four years.

LAKE BOLSENA, THE ETRUSCANS AND THEIR SUCCESSORS

THE SHORES OF LAKE BOLSENA have seen a long succession of different peoples: the Etruscans, the Romans, the northern tribes and then the people of the Middle Ages. Each period has left its mark on the landscape and the architecture of the neighbouring towns.

Situated in northern Lazio, in the volcanic complex of Vulsinio, Bolsena is the largest lake of volcanic origin in Europe. The fishing boats, which have remained the same since ancient times, remind me a little of the ones in Venice, where the fishermen, standing up and facing forwards, use asymmetrical oars: the forward oar is propulsive, while the rear one also acts as a rudder.

From the tenth century BC the Etruscans, a people of eastern stock, began settling in central Italy, first between the Tyrrhenian Sea and the Rivers Arno and Tiber, then spreading further, imposing themselves on and then integrating themselves with the less evolved native populations. They excelled in metalwork, in making weapons, in the arts, in navigation, in hydraulic engineering and in construction. They were organized in groups of 12 cities, each ruled by a figure called a Lucumon. The Lucumones met once a year in a temple known as the Fanum Voltumne, close to Lake Bolsena.

The oldest city was probably Tarquinia, founded in the eighth century BC, and the Etruscan civilization reached its peak about 200 years later. Then came a slow decline and around the third century BC, as the Romans began to expand northwards, the Etruscan cities fell one by one. Their populations were transferred to a more defensible site, not far from modern Bolsena.

When the Romans took possession of the huge wealth of the city of Velzna, on the site of the present-day Orvieto, the Roman historian Pliny the Younger reports that they took from it hundreds of gold, silver and bronze statues to adorn the Capitol. However, a few decades later these were all melted down to finance the second war against Carthage, while the broad plains along the Tyrrhenian coast were covered with the blue flowers of flax, cultivated to produce fabric for the sails of Roman warships.

The Etruscans were eventually subjugated and absorbed by the Romans with the result that no Etruscan cities have survived intact, all having been destroyed or adapted by later inhabitants. Nevertheless some constructions have survived, including numerous necropolises excavated in the tufa stone. The tombs reproduce the settings in which the dead had lived and contain personal objects for the continuation of life, based on their religious beliefs. Vases and frescoes feature in the tombs, their illustrations providing far more information than any written texts – not least because the Etruscan language remains a mystery. The wellbeing of these people, their spirituality and their perceived superiority to earthly things can be divined in the ironic smiles that illuminate their faces. To honour the deceased, they organized funeral rites as great spectacles in which the partici-pants walked in procession wearing masks of their ancestors and then carried out theatrical performances when they reached the tomb. This custom survived in Latin culture for a few centuries, so that the funeral rites for Vespasian, who died in AD 79, included a performance that re-enacted the deeds of the deceased emperor.

The minority religion of Christianity began to spread during the later days of the Roman Empire. To escape persecution the Christians would meet secretly in catacombs, some of them near the lake. It was in Bolsena, under Emperor Diocletian around 300 BC, that the young Christina was martyred; she was later canonized and made the patron saint of the city, and every year the sufferings to which she was subjected were re-lived in performance.

With the end of the Western Roman Empire in the fifth century AD the Dark Ages began, as various 'barbarian' peoples, starting with the Ostrogoths, invaded the Italian peninusla, settled and became rulers. From the seventh century, after the death of the prophet Mahomet, Islam spread throughout the Mediterranean. In the succeeding centuries, this area of the Tyrrhenian coast was continually plundered by Saracen pirates, with the inhabitants being put to the sword or enslaved. A network of look-out towers was constructed, but to no avail, and people left their homes for the hills inland, and often on the two islands on Lake Bolsena.

PREVIOUS PAGE: A panoramic view of
the 'eternal city'.
OPPOSITE: The Castel Sant' Angelo,
together with the bridge of the
same name, was originally built
as a funeral monument of the
emperors; it then became a
fortress and, since the thirteenth
century, it has been the property
of the Vatican.

The historian Suetonius has given us a portrait of Caesar in his years of maturity, presenting him as a real human being rather than a figure of legend: 'He is said to have been tall, well-proportioned and of fair complexion. His face was too full and his eyes were black and lively. He enjoyed excellent health, but in later years suffered from fainting fits and nocturnal nightmares: twice, while he was carrying out his duties, he suffered epileptic seizures.' Caesar had a strong personality and wide interests, and was highly versatile. But there were some strange quirks to his character: as a young man he faced wolves and wild boar with great courage, but he was terrified of insects, lizards and mice. Nevertheless, he had great charisma, and succeeded in all kinds of activities and glorious enterprises. His military exploits extended Roman rule over the whole of Gaul. He drove the Swabians into Germany, subdued the Belgians and landed in Britain shortly after 50 BC. In 60 BC, with Pompey and Crassus, he had formed a triumvirate to rule the Empire, but the delicate balance of power was destroyed seven years later on the death of Crassus. Pompey sought greater authority for himself, leaving Caesar no alternative but rebellion. With the support of his army he returned immediately from Gaul, of which he was governor. On the night of 10 January 49 BC he crossed the River Rubicon, beyond which no Roman general was permitted to bring his troops in peacetime, and pronounced the historic words: 'The die is cast.' It was civil war.

Subsequently, having been defeated by Caesar, Pompey fled to Egypt where Ptolemy XIV had him treacherously killed – to the genuine sorrow of Caesar. After occupying Italy and the adjacent islands, Caesar sailed to Egypt. He ousted Ptolemy and handed over the reins of power to Cleopatra, with whom he was in love.

In 45 BC, after proclaiming himself dictator for life, he reorganized the legislation, planned major public works and issued decrees on the running of the Empire and of the city, including new traffic regulations that have resonances today. For example, carts were banned within the city walls between dawn and late afternoon. Those who came to Rome in the daytime had to stop at the gates of the city and proceed on foot or hire a litter. After Caesar's time the road system evolved from century to century, and by the Middle Ages the streets were more usually circular than straight. Traffic was subject to numerous precise regulations: for example, a pedestrian had to give way to a person on horseback, a person on horseback to a cart, and an empty cart to a loaded one. But carts always had to stop and give way to men who were being chased, whether on foot or on horseback. It seems that in the eighteenth century a horse-drawn vehicle could cross the city centre at a speed of 17 kilometres per hour, whereas nowadays at rush hour Rome's buses are lucky to make an average of 6 kilometres per hour.

Traffic remains a perennial problem. As my friend Bruno says, 'I've lived in Rome for years and I ought to be used to it by now. Once I was waiting for the traffic lights to turn green, when a stream of cars overtook me on the right, with their wheels on the grass, almost in a ditch. Who did they think I was? Part of the landscape or Trajan's Column, stuck there in front

of the Parliament building? But my wife is Roman and she told me to stay cool, so I crawled meekly forward, a metre at a time, further towards the traffic intersection, where the lights had turned red again. And then I noticed, in my rear-view mirror, a Porsche that had pulled out and was overtaking the whole line of cars. That was just too much! So I swung open my door, just in front of the Porsche. A screech of brakes and then a hail of insults. I turned round to the driver and then as naturally as anything heard myself say … well, sorry but I just had to spit!' Spitting to clear one's throat is perfectly acceptable to some types of people in Italy.

Caesar's state reforms included the extending of Roman citizenship, a highly valued status that he now granted to the Gauls of Italy beyond the Po; a major colonization plan both within Italy and beyond; and the restriction of certain revels such as the famous Bacchanals. Dedicated to the cult of Bacchus, the god of wine, these were orgiastic night-time feasts where party-goers drank something called mulsum – grape must with honey. The women dyed their lips with juice from black grapes and an extract derived from a blue-flowered shrub. The senatorial decree forbidding these riotous orgies was widely ignored, despite the death sentence it supposedly carried.

The official (pre-Christian) Roman religion was a social and political fact of life: people were expected to take part in the rites as a kind of public duty, confirming and consolidating the hierarchy within the community. But there was no sense of any real connection between the faithful and the gods. Such a religion could not respond to people's inner spiritual needs

ABOVE: Pizza is now a favourite in many countries. I was starving when I ate this Roman one. In Naples the pizzas were really delicious – they say it is the city's water that makes the difference. OPPOSITE: Dining al fresco in the Trastevere district. Trastevere is a corruption of *trans Tiberim*, beyond the Tiber. Ancient Rome was founded on the left bank of the Tiber, yet residents of Trastevere, on the other side, consider themselves true Romans, *romani de' Roma*, as well.

and so unofficial mystery cults began to spring up, celebrated in private confraternities with no distinction of sex or class. People would come into contact with the divine through a state of trance, which often led them to all sorts of excesses. As the Roman historian Livy recounts, these involved orgiastic dances and acts of violence, sometimes culminating in rape or murder.

The richer private homes as well as the public baths and spas were made comfortable in winter with hypocaust heating: hot air from a furnace was made to circulate, through pierced bricks, in hollow spaces dug out under the floor and within the walls. But in the poorer parts of the city, in damp and insanitary areas, the inhabitants were often struck down by fevers. They attributed this sickness to the curses of a cruel goddess, whom they tried to ingratiate with sacrifices of all kinds. But when it was a question of toothache they turned not to a god but to a less conventional remedy: they would tie a frog to their jaw.

The ancient Romans paved their roads, but during the Middle Ages this practice fell into disuse until the thirteenth century when the people of Rome began once again to lay the streets of their city with stone, and in the next century laws were passed that made it obligatory for citizens to sweep the streets in front of their own homes. A proper street-cleaning service did not come into operation anywhere else in Europe until the seventh century.

In ancient Rome there were 40 different varieties of pear trees, some of them capable of producing fruit that weighed up to half a kilo. When a legion set up camp on conquered territory and it was presumed that they would be there for some time they would plant lettuce, the soldiers' favourite vegetable; in Britain, Spain and France it still grows in the wild today. It was the Romans who invented the *pinzimonio*, a dish of crudités comprising vegetables such as *misticanza* (various salads), celery, rucola or *puntarelle* (a type of chicory) to be dipped in oil, pepper and salt. And like the Roman legionaries themselves, the typical dishes of Rome were of humble origin, using the leftover parts of an animal that the rich would have rejected: tail, intestines, offal and cheek. The ordinary people claimed proudly that 'the more you spend, the worse you eat'. Having to make do with the innards rather than the choice cuts forced them to develop their inventive powers.

But in smart society, of course, tastes could afford to be more sophisticated. In the Empire's heyday and in the years of its long decline the wealthier Romans distinguished themselves by their Lucullan feasts – which is to say, feasts as opulent and extravagant as those hosted by the super-rich soldier–statesman Lucullus. Eventually in the sixteenth century, after the pomp of the early Renaissance, the Roman Church embarked on the Counter-Reformation as a response to Martin Luther's Protestantism, which had seized the religious imagination of much of northern Europe and was taking souls away from Catholicism. It was decided that worldliness, pleasure and excessive display should be banned, and the gates of the Vatican should remain open only to those nobles who were prepared to renounce luxury. As a result, simple dishes became common at all levels of society.

THE TAVERNS, INNS AND *TRATTORIE* 'outside the gates' and in Trastevere are the places to go to if you want to find real Roman cooking or *piatti romani de' Roma*: dishes such as *gnocchi alla romana* and *fettuccine alla romana*, both with a sauce made from dried mushrooms, chicken giblets, ham and cheese; *bucatini all'amatriciana*, with bacon, tomatoes, onion and garlic; *spaghetti alla carrettiera*, with tuna fish, mushrooms and tomatoes; *spaghetti alla carbonara,* so called because, with its sauce of readily available *guanciale* (pig's cheek), ewes'-milk cheese and egg yolk, it was an easy meal for people who worked in the woods, like the *carbonari* or charcoal burners; the simple *pasta ajo e ojo* (or *aglio e olio*), pasta with garlic and oil; and *abbacchio*, a very young lamb referred to by the Roman poet Juvenal as the 'tenderest of the flock'.

For many centuries the region of Lazio was given over to pasture, and when Juvenal invited his friend Persicus to visit him at his villa in Tivoli he told him they would eat goat 'so tender that it had not yet grazed its first grass' and so was 'fuller of milk than of blood', wild asparagus picked on the mountain by a peasant girl, eggs

POPULAR ROMAN COOKING AND THE ABBACCHIO

taken still warm from the henhouse, and fruit from the orchard. Good ingredients cooked with no fuss or frills, using simple country recipes.

Let's see what this *abbacchio alla romana* is all about. Take a boned leg of young spring lamb (get your butcher to bone it for you), plain flour, some unsalted, boned anchovies, olive oil, garlic, salt, pepper, some of the small hot peppers known as *peperoncini* (outside the Mediterranean, a jar from an Italian delicatessen may be your best bet), fresh rosemary, sage leaves, white wine (if possible a dry one from the region of the Castelli Romani), white wine vinegar and potatoes. Cut the boned leg into bite-sized pieces and coat them in flour. Put a couple of anchovies in a frying pan with some oil, adding a chopped clove of garlic. Let the garlic brown lightly, then put the *abbacchio* in the pan, season with salt and pepper, and add some *peperoncini*, some sprigs of rosemary and a couple of sage leaves. Sauté the pieces of

lamb quickly on a high heat until brown, turning them continually to make sure that they soak up all the flavour and don't burn. Then pour in the wine mixed with vinegar and let it evaporate almost completely before adding a ladleful of boiling water: the meat mustn't burn, but neither must the sauce be too liquid – midway, as the Romans used to say, '*In medium stat virtus*'. To round things off add the potatoes, peeled and sliced. Then you can either place the whole thing in a casserole dish in a medium oven for a good half-hour, or put a lid on the pan and finish cooking the lamb on a low flame. If the sauce gets too dry, add some hot water mixed with vinegar. Finally transfer the lamb to a heated serving dish and serve very hot. Although the *abbachio* is cooked in white wine, accompany it with a full-bodied red.

There are various versions of this dish such as *coratella d'abbacchio* and roast *abbacchio* or *alla cacciatora*. And not to be forgotten is *saltimbocca*, slices of veal rolled up with sage and ham, pinned together with a toothpick to provide the shape that the name evokes (literally, 'leap into the mouth'), then cooked in butter and Marsala.

RIGHT: The Forum. The columns on the right are the remains of the Temple of Saturn, the triumphal arch in the centre is the Arch of Septimus Severus and the three columns to the left are all that is left of the Temple of Vespasian.

The Roman love of sweet dishes can be traced back to the eating habits of the Catholic cardinals; chocolate was produced using recipes created in convents and monasteries, whose occupants were far from impervious to the temptations of the dinner table. But the question arose as to whether chocolate, which came to Europe with the return of Christopher Columbus from the New World at the turn of the sixteenth century, should be considered a fat or a lean food – whether, that is to say, it should be allowed or not in Lent. And so at the end of the seventeenth century a cardinal published an essay in which, to the joy of his fellow-churchmen, he established that chocolate was a lean food and could be eaten even in periods of penitence. Religious traditions also gave us liqueurs, like those of the Trappist monks who invented extracts of eucalyptus and other herbal drinks, such as *elixir imperiale* based on anise.

But such soft living was not the lot of men of action, either then or in ancient times. Around 50 BC, Julius Caesar was able to carry out his reforms and to establish Roman rule abroad thanks to the unparalleled power he wielded – a power based both on his moral ascendancy and on the army, in which every legionary was an expert warrior. Each soldier carried not only his own weapons but also sufficient basic rations to survive several days. He could hit a target with a javelin from a distance of about 25 metres – the best ones could manage it from 40 metres. But in the centuries that followed, these skills proved inadequate to prevent the fall of the Roman Empire. The infantry-based Romans could do nothing to defeat the powerful cavalry of the barbarian invaders.

Caesar respected the political power of the people and refused to allow himself any special privileges. One day he had a servant put in irons because he had given better bread to him than to his guests. He thought it was important to guarantee administrative justice in the 18 provinces of the Empire, and, through legislation, to eliminate all abuses by local functionaries. Nevertheless on 15 March 44 BC a group of conspirators, led by Brutus and Cassius, stabbed him to death in the Senate because they believed his power had grown too great for comfort.

Numerous coins were minted to commemorate the death of Caesar, showing the date, a Phrygian cap (gladiator's helmet) and two gladiator's swords. He had been born in Rome in

100 BC, a member of the authoritative Gens Giulia, in the quarter of Suburra, which became the Monti district. Together with Trastevere it was always considered the most important district of the city, and its inhabitants still claim to be descendants of the ancient Romans. In these two districts you used to find the strongest and sturdiest men in Rome – as well as the most beautiful women. However, marriages between the two districts were rare, since people were supposed to choose a partner from within their own area. The leaders of the two districts were always rivals: there were often dawn encounters with knives to decide who was the number one tough guy, and what were known as the 'stone-throwing fights in the Cow Field' were notorious.

Until the early 1800s the area around the ruins of the old Roman Forum was known as the Cow Field, because cows and sheep were left to graze there. Among their herdsmen there was a long-standing tradition of off-the-cuff poetry: verses in *ottava rima* – 8 lines of 11 syllables each, with a fixed rhyming pattern – on chivalrous or topical themes, which were improvised in taverns or at local fairs. The poets had often had little schooling but knew by heart such classics as Ariosto's epic *Orlando Furioso* or Dante's *Divine Comedy*, which they would read over and over again while out alone with their flocks.

It was not until the nineteenth century that any value began to be attributed to Rome's buried archaeological heritage. The German writer Goethe's words on this subject, written during his journey in Italy, are memorable:

> *I am growing familiar with the topography of ancient and new Rome, I observe ruins and buildings, I explore this or that villa, I slowly approach the most beautiful sights and all I can do is open my eyes and stare as I wander around, since it is only in Rome that one can prepare oneself to understand Rome. But it must be admitted that it is a hard and saddening task to dig out the ancient, piece by piece, in new Rome; and yet one must do it, trusting in the unparalleled satisfaction to be gained. Everywhere are traces of magnificence and decay that are equally beyond our imagination. What the barbarians respected, the builders of new Rome have devastated.*

It was at the end of the fifteenth century that there took place what Goethe referred to as a 'constant, methodical and brutal spoliation', to obtain materials for the buildings that were being created in the fervour of the Renaissance. And from this time onwards many other valuable objects were dispersed throughout the art markets of the world.

When I was working at Cinecittà, Rome's film studios, I lived in Via Madonna dei Monti in the Monti district and, on my way home from a long day's work, I loved to get lost in its streets. There was one in particular that used to inspire my imagination, Via Panisperna, site of some of the most important scientific discoveries of the twentieth century.

IN AUTUMN 1926 the physicist Enrico Fermi moved to Rome, to the Institute of Physics in the Via Panisperna, where he was given the first chair in theoretical physics in Italy and attracted a group of similar-minded scientists. Like other great physicists before him, Fermi always ensured a close link between theory and experimentation in his research activities. Study grants had already taken him to Germany and Holland. In Leyden he had met Einstein, and in 1925, having heard of Wolfgang Pauli's 'exclusion principle', he discovered, in addition to the particles at half-integer spin, electrons, protons and neutrons, other particles within the atom that obeyed this principle. These are now known as fermions, and the discovery had made him internationally famous.

The work of the 'Via Panisperna boys' continued and in the 1930s, after discovering the resonant absorption of neutrons by certain nuclei, Fermi formulated the theory of the slowing of neutrons. It contained many of the physical ideas and mathematical methods that underlie the theory of nuclear reactors, and in 1938 he was awarded the Nobel Prize for Physics.

One of the 'boys' was a brilliant mathematician called Ettore Maiorana who, shortly before World War II, simply disappeared into thin air. Fermi described him in these words: 'From a distance he appeared lanky, with an awkward gait; from close up one noticed his very black hair, his dark complexion, slightly sunken cheeks, dark flashing eyes: all together he looked like a Saracen.' On Maiorana's first

THE MATHEMATICIAN WHO DISAPPEARED

day at the institute Fermi had shown him the statistical model he was elaborating, now known as the Thomas–Fermi model. Next day Maiorana turned up in Fermi's office with a piece of paper and asked to see the numerical table with the solution. By hand, and in just one day, he had solved the equation that Fermi had been working on with a rudimentary calculator for weeks. Maiorana claimed he wished to check the correctness of Fermi's calculations, since he was perfectly sure of his own.

As a child prodigy, at the age of three Maiorana used to hide underneath the table 'out of embarrassment' when he was given complicated sums to do, like extracting square roots or doing

long multiplications. Now, as an adult, he felt able to display these skills, such as challenging Fermi to little contests of skill in calculation – but he still felt uneasy about his prowess and preferred to turn his face to the wall. Fermi felt no rivalry. On the contrary, he was enthusiastic about Maiorana: 'There are various categories of scientists in this world; second- and third-rate people, who do their best but never get far. Then there are the first-rate people, who make discoveries of great importance. But after that come the geniuses, like Galileo and Newton. Well, Ettore was one of these.' Fermi and 'the boys' would go looking, while Maiorana would simply find.

Maiorana had a keen sense of irony and a critical spirit that earned him the name of 'Grand Inquisitor' in Via Panisperna. But in those days he was also lively and sociable, meeting up with his companions in the afternoon in the Villa Borghese Gardens or at the Caffè Faraglino. Nor was he a single-track genius: he was also widely read in philosophy and literature, from Schopenhauer to Pirandello.

It was not until 1933 that Maiorana became the grim and solitary scientist of legend. After returning from a period of research in Germany he began to isolate himself, working alone at home and paying little attention to his personal appearance; despite his protests, someone sent a barber to his house. Some thought he might have become politicized in Germany, where Hitler had just come to power. It is quite possible that Maiorana, who had been taken up by the 'nationalist' Werner Heisenberg while studying in Leipzig, shared the German physicist's dramatic political vision. However, he was certainly not attracted by Nazism.

Towards the end of 1937 Maiorana was appointed professor emeritus, as had happened with Guglielmo Marconi, at the University of Naples 'for the fame he has achieved of singular expertise'. He devoted himself keenly to teaching. But in the late thirties, with the European dictators confronting the democratic nations, Maiorana must have realized that war was inevitable and that physicists would have to take a position: he could not remain neutral. His character had now become introverted, sullen, peevish, uncommunicative and perfectionist: in his opinion physics was taking the wrong path. And suddenly, after years of intense study but also of apparent scientific isolation, despite the fame he had achieved he decided to 'disappear'.

On 25 March 1938 Maiorana gave a file of his manuscripts to his best student, a woman,

saying: 'You keep them. We'll talk about it later.' But those manuscripts, of the greatest importance for physics, somehow got lost. He took his passport and withdrew his money from the bank. In his room in the Hotel Bologna in Naples he left an envelope containing a short message to his family: 'I just have one wish: that you shouldn't wear black for me. If you want to follow the conventions, wear some sign of mourning, but for no longer than three days. Afterwards, remember me, if you can, in your hearts and forgive me.'

He then wrote a farewell letter to the director of the Physics Institute of Naples before embarking on the ferry to Palermo. From there he sent a second letter on Hotel Sole letterhead, saying: 'The sea refused me and I'll return to the Hotel Bologna, maybe travelling together with this same sheet of paper.'

The letters, in neat, precise handwriting, were confused and ambiguous yet appeared to have some kind of underlying purpose: they seemed to

reflect the scheme of his actual 'disappearance', based on the two-way trip he was taking, in a state of psychological uncertainty. In choosing the Hotel Bologna perhaps he was alluding to his uncle, who was an anti-relativist physicist and was due to see Hitler on his way through the city of Bologna; Hotel Sole is possibly a reference to Japan, the land of the rising sun.

On the ferry back the other passenger who occupied his cabin was perhaps Maiorana himself, using the false name of Carlo Price. A scientist named James Price had poisoned himself at the age of 31 after challenging London's Royal Society, of which he was a member, on the subject of the alchemical trans-mutation of mercury into gold. He claimed to have done so, but he refused to repeat the experiment in front of an academic audience. Maybe Maiorana wanted to let his relatives know that he had not taken his own life; they did indeed reach this conclusion, since no body was ever found in the sea. Some have even speculated that Maiorana retired to the same monastery in Argentina as the pilot who some seven years later dropped the atomic bomb on Hiroshima.

As for Fermi, he settled in America after anti-Semitic legislation made it unwise for his Jewish wife to stay in Italy. He continued his research and eventually joined the Manhattan Project, which was responsible for developing the atomic bomb – that terrible weapon of destruction. Perhaps it was fear of that kind of involvement that made his Via Panisperna colleague decide to disappear.

OPPOSITE: Ettore Maiorana, the brilliant mathematician.
LEFT: Enrico Fermi, the illustrious physicist.

The street contains, from much earlier times, the remains of the Domus Aurea, which Emperor Nero had built on the Oppian Hill; it consists of about 150 rooms arranged around an octagon that forms the hub of the whole complex. The Domus Aurea arose on the ashes of the fire of AD 64, which destroyed most of Rome while Nero watched, playing on his lyre and singing of the fall of Troy. His impressive residence occupied nearly the entire centre of the city and included a lake 'almost as vast as a sea'. The only places comparable in terms of size and luxury are the great palaces of oriental dynasties or those of the court of Alexandria, and it was from their ideologies that Nero derived his own absolutist vision of imperial power. He had himself represented in the likeness of the sun god in the famous bronze statue of the Colossus, over 35 metres high; this was placed in the vestibule of the new house, on the spot where the Emperor Hadrian would later build the Temple of Venus.

Around AD 118 Hadrian had his own colossal villa built not far from Rome, near the slopes of the Tiburtine Mountains south-west of Tivoli. The perfect harmony between architecture and landscape make the Villa Hadriana an exception in the history of ancient building. Beneath the villa is a network of underground roads, some of them wide enough for carriages, others only for pedestrians. It meant that servants and slaves could go about their business without interfering with the activities of the privileged one level above.

Rome itself has its own underground city: the catacombs. These underground cemeteries used by Christian communities originated in the second century AD and continued to be dug until the first half of the fifth century. In conformity with Roman laws, which prohibited burials within the walls of the city, all the catacombs are situated in the suburbs and along the great roads that lead out of Rome. The Christians

rejected the pagan custom of cremation; taking their example from the burial of Christ they preferred inhumation, awaiting the day of Resurrection. This created a potential problem: if they had confined themselves to open-air cemeteries, without reusing existing tombs, they would soon have run out of space; so the catacombs solved the problem economically, practically and securely. The Christians gathered in the catacombs to celebrate funeral rites, the anniversaries of their martyrs and the dead. During the persecutions these underground chambers served as places of temporary refuge for the celebration of the Eucharist. When the persecutions finished, around AD 300, the catacombs became sanctuaries dedicated to martyrs, centres of devotion and pilgrimage from every part of the Roman Empire.

In addition to the catacombs and the numerous other underground sites of ancient and medieval Rome, there are now all the subterranean entrails of the modern city. Out in the countryside west of the capital stands the E42 building, or Palazzo della Civiltà Italiana, constructed to house the universal exhibition planned for 1942, the twentieth anniversary of Mussolini's march on Rome. (The idea did not prove a very bright one, as war broke out before the exhibition could be held.) Beneath the building, 8 metres below street level, is a hollow prism of cement.

OPPOSITE: At Hadrian's Villa, 28 kilometres east of Rome, Apollo stands over the Canopus, an elongated lake. Excavations were begun here in the fifteenth century under Pope Pius II.
ABOVE: Villa Lante, the consummate example of one of the finest periods in the history of garden design – the Mannerist phase of the Italian Renaissance.

129

You feel you are entering a submarine, but it is in fact a gigantic bunker. It was built for Mussolini, and equipped with every possible facility. On the walls are notices suggesting suitable behaviour in an emergency situation: 'Keep Calm', 'Silence'. In one room stand two tandem bicycles, bolted to the floor and connected by wires to an electric panel. Their rear wheels have been replaced by metal discs, for this is a dynamo to produce and store the energy produced by the pedals. It powers the emergency ventilation system, to be used in the event of a power cut.

It was a pilot building, and the intention was to reproduce it in a network of tunnels almost 20 kilometres long. The site, which was then crossed by the Via Imperiale, is laid out in the form of a long, narrow pentagon oriented towards the sea. In April 1937 the project had already been planned down to the last detail, but it was only completed in the 1960s. It is a synthesis of rationalism and monumentality, inspired more by the surrealist paintings of De Chirico than by Greek and Roman canons, with lavish use of marble to coat the reinforced concrete.

Some years ago a Roman entrepreneur, terrified by the idea of nuclear war, decided to build an atomic-bombproof bunker in the garden of his country house. He contacted a local building firm, which stipulated a construction using a highly resistant form of pre-compressed reinforced concrete and tempered steel. The commission was completed quickly, though expensively, but then one of the builder's lorries bumped into a corner of it and the whole thing collapsed like a house of cards. The investigators said the sand had been added to the mix carelessly and the 'bombproof bunker' wouldn't even have stood up to a strong gust of wind.

In the 1930s, during the Fascist period, a new town was built on an area of drained marsh-land south of Rome. Sabaudia was intended to be the ideal urban development: rationalist architecture in harmony with the landscape. It looks on to the Tyrrhenian Sea, the same sea in which Ulysses gave up his travels for love of the sorceress Circe, whose mythical profile appears as if stretched out on the crest of Monte Circeo. Now the beach is lined with villas that once belonged to famous names such as the writer Alberto Moravia, the film director Pier Paolo Pasolini and the actress Anita Ekberg – the star, with Marcello Mastroianni, of Fellini's *La Dolce Vita*. This film offers a perfect picture of Rome in the late 1950s and early 1960s, the years when you would go to Sabaudia to meet platinum blondes in flowered bikinis and sandals, with names like Orsetta, Lavinia or Denise.

CHURCH AND STATE

After AD 313 Christians no longer needed to meet clandestinely in catacombs, for in that year the Emperor Constantine converted to Christianity, which subsequently became the state religion. The Church soon began to receive generous gifts and bequests, and within a few years it was a major financial power. The Bishop of Rome – the Pope – was recognized as the legitimate successor of the apostle Peter, who had been martyred in Rome.

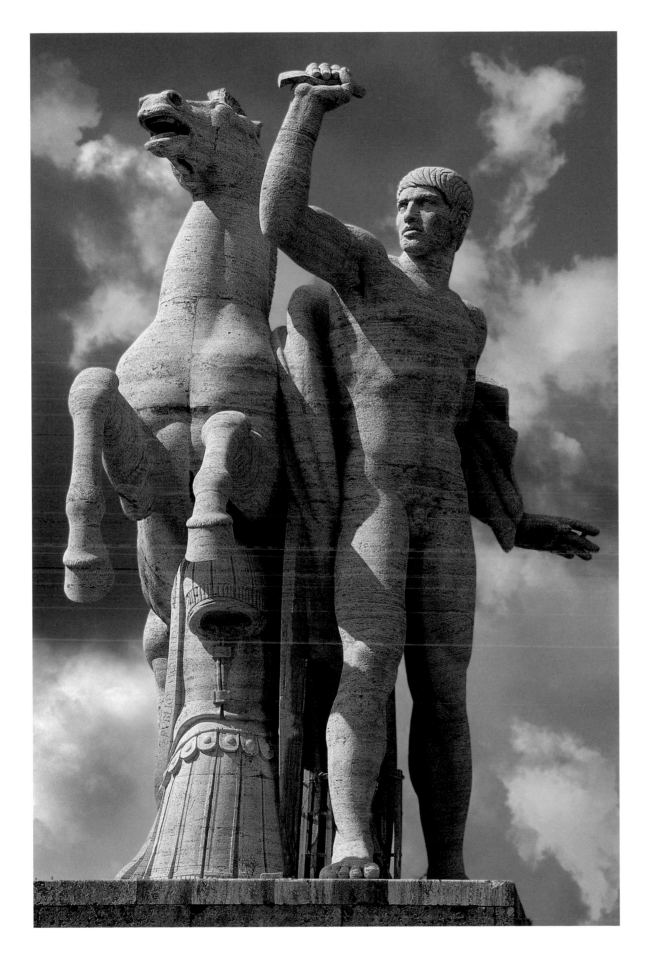

In 395 the Roman Empire was split into the Roman Empire of the East, of Greek descent, with Constantinople as its capital, and the Roman Empire of the West, with Rome as its capital. The latter ceased to exist in 476 when the last emperor, Romulus Augustus, was deposed by Odoacer, leader of the barbarian armies that had descended from northern and eastern Europe. However, Rome as the centre of the then known world showed no sign of declining but grew ever stronger because of the Pope and the power wielded by the Church. When Gregory I became Pope, around the end of the sixth century, he consolidated the primacy of the Bishop of Rome as the supreme judge in religious, dogmatic and disciplinary matters, reinforcing the great hierarchical organization throughout Europe that depended on the Church of Rome.

Subsequently the popes, anxious to free themselves both from the feeble tutelage of Constantinople and from the pressure exerted by the Lombards, who had invaded Italy in 568 and now ruled much of it from Milan, sought foreign assistance. They went to the Franks, addressing their pleas to Pepin the Short (son of Charles Martel, who had blocked the Arabs' attempt to overrun France), whom the papacy had supported in a recent Frankish power struggle. The grateful King Pepin and his army duly forced the Lombards to hand over to the Church substantial territory including the castles of Sutri, Nepi, Ameria, Bomarzo and Orte. Pepin was succeeded on his death by his son Charlemagne, who came down into Italy from France with his armies and in 773 put an end to the kingdom of the Lombards.

On Christmas Day 800 Pope Leo III crowned Charlemagne Holy Roman Emperor – successor to the earlier (Western) emperors who had ruled from Rome. This gave him the same status as the other Christian emperor in Constantinople. But the holders of the latter office were not always up to the mark. Later that century Emperor Theophilus, an authoritarian ruler who had gone bald, issued an edict ordering all men to shave their heads on pain of death.

Charlemagne, who had won the respect and obedience of his feudal vassals, was the effective temporal leader of the Church, with the Pope as religious head. The Carolingian dynasty seemed to be in a very secure position. But on Charlemagne's death his son Louis, known as 'the Good', lost control of the vassals and three years later the Empire was divided up among his own sons, with a good deal of squabbling over the share-out. The Empire fell into a serious crisis and in 887 Charles 'the Fat' was deposed. These wranglings severely undermined the power of the Church; it seems that Pope John VIII, who had succeeded in 872, was actually murdered in 882 by some conspirators who first poisoned him and then hacked him to death. The break-up of the Carolingian Empire resulted in two separate states, one French and one German, which would continue to fight over possession of Italy. Meanwhile, the popes exploited this rivalry to play the French off against the Germans and vice versa, depending on the changing circumstances.

After being elected to the papacy in 891, Pope Formosus called the German King Arnulf to Rome and crowned him emperor in opposition to the other candidate, Lambert of Spoleto. On the death of Formosus the Spoletans, seeking redress, persuaded his successor Stephen VI,

OPPOSITE: The collection of monsters at Bomarzo includes this ogre, with its huge head, wide open eyes and screaming mouth. The park was devised by the architect Pirro Ligorio, who completed St Peter's Cathedral in Rome after the death of Michelangelo and built the Villa d'Este at Tivoli.

AT THE END OF THE EIGHTEENTH CENTURY British writers invented the Gothic horror novel: stories of gloomy castles, sinister counts and deranged locals. For some reason, these novels were nearly always set in Italy, which evoked the same response in them as Bram Stoker's vampire-ridden vision of Transylvania did with later generations. These travellers saw crumbling ruins in wild landscapes and heard stories of mad princes and ghosts; their imaginations were fired. And if they had seen Bomarzo, who could have blamed them? This is a place of fantasy that is not quite of this world, full of grotesque monsters and nightmare creations that later inspired the surrealist artist Salvador Dali to make a film here.

BOMARZO: IMAGINATION RUN RIOT

In the sixteenth century a hunch-backed duke called Vicino Orsini ruled these parts. A great warrior, he had a beautiful wife named Giulia who tamed his heart. When she died he was devastated and from then on devoted his time to creating his 'Sacred Wood of Bomarzo', a parody of the pretentious artistic trends of the time, which he dedicated to his wife's memory.

These words are written at the entrance to the wood: 'You, who roam the world in search of sublime and fearful wonders, come hither and look upon terrible countenances, elephants, lions, bears, man-eaters and dragons.' The place is packed with extraordinary statues whose symbolic significance is uncertain, although some of them seem to relate to the contemporary poet Ariosto's epic on the madness of the medieval warrior hero Roland, *Orlando Furioso*. The park of Bomarzo is a kind of mystery in stone, connected in some way with madness and love and Duke Orsini's own grief at Giulia's death. At the top of the Sacred Wood is a memorial to her, a temple of divine love. It is best, however, not to try too hard to interpret *everything* here, but simply to experience it.

who supported their side, to order the body to be exhumed: the corpse was subjected to a trial and finally thrown into the Tiber. There were other popes who came to worse ends. Medieval chronicles tell of a woman who became pope under the name of John VIII (not to be confused with the other Pope John VIII, who acceded in 872). She is said to have been a noblewoman of English origin, although born in Mainz in Germany. Having fallen in love with a Benedictine monk and followed him to Rome, disguised as a man, she too became a monk under the name of Johannes Anglicus. In an age when the method of selecting popes was somewhat haphazard, she acceded to this office on the death of Leo IV in 855.

During the Easter procession the crowd clustered tightly around the papal horse and the animal shied. The new Pope was in fact pregnant, and the trauma sent her into labour. Those who had rushed forward to render assistance were flabbergasted when 'Pope Joan', as she was later known, gave birth to a baby boy. No pity was shown. Joan and her newborn baby were stoned; then the two bodies, after being tied to the tails of horses and dragged around in front of the crowd, were buried in unconsecrated ground.

After that, great care was taken with the selection procedures: 'to prevent the same mistake being committed, every time a Pope is created, he has to sit on a chair with an opening underneath him, so that the last Deacon can touch him and check that he is male'. In later centuries this story was denied by Catholics, who claimed it was all an invention of the Protestants.

After these bizarre events the papacy descended to unbelievable depths of immorality. It was torn between two factions, one linked to the Empire and the other to the Roman aristocracy. Concubinage and corruption were rife. One pope was suffocated with a pillow, and at one stage three rival popes claimed the office simultaneously, reciprocally excommunicating one another. Then, in the mid-eleventh century, the Patriarch of Constantinople left the Church of Rome in order to set up the Greek Orthodox Church.

The balance of power between popes and emperors remained delicate. Both now agreed that royal power was granted divinely, but while the emperors held that their power derived from the direct will of God, the popes claimed that only they, as representatives of God on earth, could appoint emperors. In 1073, by popular acclamation and by the will of the cardinals, Hildebrand, from Soana in Tuscany, became pope, taking the name of Gregory VII. Humble, but also tenacious and courageous, he was convinced that his authority came from Christ and he used it to moralize the Church and to reaffirm its rights over sovereigns. Daringly, he ordered that only the Roman pope could be called universal; that the pope was the only man whose feet sovereigns must kiss; that the pope could depose emperors; that nobody could condemn a decision of the apostolic see; that the Roman Church had never erred and never could err; that anyone who was not with the Roman church could not be considered Catholic; that the pope could dissolve the oath of loyalty made to unjust rulers; and that priestly dignity was superior to royal dignity. The battle between Church and State was definitely not over yet.

POPES: PATRONS OF THE ARTS BUT NOT OF SCIENCE

The Inquisition is said to have been initiated in 1234, when Pope Gregory IX issued a bull in which he spoke of the duty of 'capturing the little foxes, the heretics that are hidden in the tortuous dens of Burgundy intent on destroying the Lord's vineyard, and to extirpate them from there once and for all'. For several centuries this powerful organization within the Church would exert its authority, often with enormous cruelty, to stamp out all deviation.

It was in 1300 that the first holy year was proclaimed. The number of pilgrims that flocked to Rome from many lands for this celebration confirmed the centrality of both city and papacy to the Christian world. From 1305 to 1377 the seat of the papacy was forcibly moved by the French to Avignon; a situation prolonged for a further 50 years in France by the appointment of a number of 'opposition' claimants known as anti-popes.

In the fifteenth century the structure of Rome was radically transformed. Humanistic culture emerged from the small circle of Renaissance artists and men of letters: through architecture, works of art and new ideas concerning the 'ideal city', humanism eventually conquered even ecclesiastical circles all the way up to the popes. It was they who were principally responsible for the new appearance of Rome; they built and decorated churches and palaces, effectively redesigning the city, which they wanted to make once again the most impressive in the world. To celebrate the holy year of 1475 Sixtus V improved the city's road system, commissioning the first new bridge across the Tiber since ancient times, the Ponte Sisto.

The sixteenth century opened with the papacy of Julius II, who created two new riverside streets, the Via Giulia and the Via della Lungara, and who summoned to his service great artists and architects such as Leon Battista Alberti, Donato Bramante, Benvenuto Cellini, Michelangelo and Raphael. At the end of 1508 Raphael began to paint a great cycle of frescoes on the walls of

BELOW: Situated in the cloister of San Pietro in Montorio, the Tempietto is a seminal building in the history of architecture. It was designed by Bramante at the beginning of the sixteenth century.

the *Stanze* (rooms) in the Vatican. He became engaged to the niece of a cardinal, but could never bring himself to marry her. It seems that the painter was torn between his ambition to become a cardinal, a position from which married men were precluded, and his devotion to amorous pleasures. It is said that Maria, his fiancée, died of a broken heart as the marriage continued to be postponed; the artist died shortly afterwards at the age of 37, as a result of continual fevers. After their death the two were finally united, buried side by side in the Pantheon.

It was Michelangelo whom Julius II entrusted with the task of decorating the Sistine Chapel, where for the first time the artist's doctrinal conception was expressed. The chapel took its name from Pope Sixtus IV della Rovere who had it restructured, redecorating it with *trompe l'oeil* hangings depicting the stories of Moses and Christ, and portraits of the popes. The day after his nephew, Julius II, was elected pope, he started to efface the memory of the hated Borgia popes: he removed their names from Vatican documents; covered the family portraits with black drapes; had their corpses exhumed and transported to Spain; and had his own residence moved to the third floor of the Vatican Palace, since the walls of the apartments that had been occupied by Alexander VI were covered with frescoes bearing the coat-of-arms of the Borgia family.

Then, more constructively, he decided to continue the work of Sixtus IV and called upon Michelangelo to paint the ceiling of the Sistine Chapel. He was supported in this by Bramante, who wanted to encourage Michelangelo to leave his current project, Julius' tomb, and to try his hand at fresco, a technique he had never attempted before. Michelangelo had been known in Vatican circles for some time: it is said that at the beginning of the sixteenth century a statue of splendid workmanship, representing a sleeping Cupid, had been dug up on the building site of a new house; it had one arm missing, but was otherwise in perfect condition. Everyone admired it as a wonderful example of the perfection of classical art. It was actually a fake created by Michelangelo – he had spent a good deal of time studying antiquities and had a profound knowledge of Greek and Roman sculpture. After carving the statue he had 'distressed' it to make it look like a relic of ancient Rome: he had removed an arm, given the figure the appearance of age and then buried it in the ground. The work was going to be sold to Cardinal Raffaele Riario, but when he heard of the deception he refused it. However, he asked to meet the artist. And from there, Michelangelo's fame spread.

Bramante was given the task of preparing the scaffolding for the frescoing of the Sistine Chapel; it was hung by ropes from the ceiling, which as a result had to be perforated in several places. Michelangelo, complaining that he couldn't work on a surface full of holes, obtained the Pope's permission to redesign the scaffolding. He showed how it could be set up, without touching the areas he was going to paint. As a great deal of rope had been bought that was no longer required, he gave it all to the carpenter who had built the scaffolding; it proved enough to pay for his daughter's dowry.

LEFT: 'The frescoes that we are contemplating here introduce us into the world of the contents of the Revelation. The truths of our faith speak to us here from all sides. From them human genius took its inspiration, undertaking to clothe them in forms of incomparable beauty.' With these words, spoken during the Holy Mass celebrated on 8 April 1994, on the completion of the restoration of the Sistine Chapel's Last Judgement, the late Pope John Paul II emphasized the sacredness of the chapel and the remarkable skill in Michelangelo's art.

OPPOSITE: St Peter's is possibly the largest church in Christendom – I nearly expired due to exhaustion when, aged 10, I climbed the spiral staircase to the top of the dome. Its magnificence has certainly provided the inspiration for many other domes around the world, including St Paul's Cathedral in London, Les Invalides in Paris, the United States Capitol in Washington DC, St Joseph's Oratory in Montreal and the more literal representation of the Basilica of Our Lady of Peace of Yamoussoukro on the Ivory Coast.

Having no experience in fresco painting, Michelangelo summoned some painters from Florence and got them to start the work. They imparted the secrets of the technique but he was not satisfied with the quality of their painting, so after a few days he decided to rework everything from scratch. He locked himself in the chapel and had the other painters turned out, both from the chapel and from his own house. They went back to Florence shamefacedly.

Both artist and patron would seem to have had personality problems. According to some, Michelangelo had inherited from his father a tendency to self-pity and hypochondria, together with a conviction that his family, the Buonarotti, were descended from a noble and ancient lineage. Julius II was not easy. He had an intimidating character, feared by all those around him on account of his violent outbursts of rage, which earned him the name of the 'Terrible Pope'. When he was angry he had no qualms about striking his subordinates, with either his fists or a stick. Relations between the two men were never easy; while working on the chapel Michelangelo often had fierce arguments with Julius, who, against the painter's wishes, wanted to see the progress of the fresco. Once Michelangelo pretended to leave Rome, but actually hid inside the chapel; when the Pope entered the artist dropped some planks from above, nearly hitting him. He had to flee, and it was only thanks to Bramante's intervention on his behalf that Michelangelo found the courage to return. But it seems that Michelangelo made his patron pay for it in the end: tired of Julius continually breathing down his neck and declaring that Michelangelo had the temper of a devil, the artist is said to have painted on the ceiling a small devil with the facial features of the Pope.

In 1512 the poet Ariosto accompanied Alfonso d'Este, Duke of Ferrara, on a visit to the Pope and was able to admire the frescoes that Michelangelo was creating. The memory of this experience is given expression in his poem *Orlando Furioso*, where the great painter and sculptor is described as '*Michel, più che mortale, angel divino*' (Michael, more than mortal, divine angel).

In October of that year the work was completed, and on All Saints' Day Julius II inaugurated the Sistine Chapel with a solemn mass. The nine central panels represent stories from the Book of Genesis, from the Creation to the Fall of Man, the Flood and the subsequent rebirth of mankind with the family of Noah. Michelangelo, drawing on his extraordinary artistic gifts, had tried to illustrate the invisible beauty and majesty of God, and, guided by the words of Genesis, he made the Sistine Chapel 'the sanctuary of the theology of the human body'. The chapel became, for the whole Catholic community, the place where the Holy Spirit operates – in particular, in the selection of the person who is to be the Bishop of Rome and the successor of St Peter. Even now, at the end of the conclave for the election of a new pope, the voting cards used by the cardinals are placed in an old stove connected to the chimney of the Sistine Chapel. On the stove are two knobs that free the substances that turn the smoke white, if the election has proved successful, and black, if unsuccessful.

In 1978, in the conclave that led to the election of John Paul I – the Patriarch of Venice, Albino Luciani – the chapel was filled with a toxic black smoke because the chimney had not been properly cleaned, and the 111 cardinals present nearly suffocated. Luciani, by whom I was confirmed in St Mark's Basilica and whom I remember for his friendliness, openness and humanity, only lived to be Pope for 33 days.

His sixteenth-century predecessor Julius II's other great project was the rebuilding of St Peter's. Bramante and Raphael seemed to subscribe to the idea that the arts could converge and blend, whereas Michelangelo felt that the synthesis of art, whether in concept or execution, was quite separate from the medium: individual techniques for the carrying out of an idea must be subordinate to the underlying intellectual principle. This artistic expression of Michelangelo's was amplified in his last work, the dome of St Peter's, a space that appears to be generated almost by centrifugal force, in which a drum shape rhythmically marked out by large windows between pairs of protruding columns gives the impression of a gigantic toothed wheel biting into the free space of the sky. The gigantic dome transforms the weight of this mass into an upward thrust via the tension of the ribs that converge towards its summit. While Brunelleschi's dome of Santa Maria del Fiore in Florence was said to have been created broad enough to cover all the peoples of Tuscany, the dome of St Peter's was to be broad enough to cover all the peoples of Christendom.

By the end of the sixteenth century the Catholic Church had grown extremely powerful. The immense wealth it had accumulated was continually flaunted, and the popes and their courts lived in great luxury; the living conditions of the masses, however, remained wretched. Strong criticism of this disparity was voiced by the Protestant Reformation led by the German priest Martin Luther.

In response, the Church tightened its control over what people thought, said, read and did. Leonardo da Vinci, who had dissected dozens of corpses for his anatomical studies, was accused of being a violator of tombs, and the Pope himself forbade him access to the mortuary chamber of the Santo Spirito. The Inquisition stepped up its activities. On 17 February 1600 the philosopher Giordano Bruno, who did not subscribe to traditional Catholic thinking and supported the Polish-born astronomer Copernicus in his belief that the earth orbited the sun, not vice versa, was burned at the stake in Campo dei Fiori. Perceived heresy had to be rooted out, no matter how terrible the means. For the first time the Roman Catholic Church had physically eliminated an adherent to a scientific theory that was anathema to it.

When Cardinal Borghese became Pope Paul V in 1605, his insistence on firm ecclesiastical jurisdiction led to strong disagreements with various cities and states within Italy. Venice, for instance, enacted a law that forbade property being transferred in favour of the clergy, and another that required the approval of the civil authorities for the construction of new churches. Two priests were sent to jail on account of this provision. As a result the Pope decided to

OPPOSITE: The Campo dei Fiori used to be covered in plants and flowers, until about the middle of the fifteenth century when the area was developed by the Church, to serve pilgrims flocking in from all over Italy who required the services of craftsmen, provisions and lodgings.

excommunicate the government of Venice and imposed an interdict on the entire city which, among other things, forbade the priests to celebrate mass and the citizens to receive the sacraments. Paul V was strict and inflexible, a lawyer rather than a diplomat, who defended the privileges of the Church with all his might. But like many other popes he was also guilty of nepotism, manipulating the rise of the Borghese family. His nephew, Cardinal Scipione Borghese, became enormously powerful, putting even the pope himself into a difficult position because he was a supporter of the artist Caravaggio.

Michelangelo Merisi, known as Caravaggio, was born in Milan in 1571 and spent his youth in a region of northern Italy, Lombardy, that was politically and artistically conservative. In 1584, at the age of 13, he was apprenticed in the workshop of a Milanese painter. Eight years later – an indication of the way his whole life would be lived – the young Merisi had to leave Milan in a hurry on account of some obscure murder case. He went to Rome. A dusty city with smelly streets and a river that often burst its banks, it nevertheless offered more lively surroundings to a young man from the staid north. Its palaces and hovels were variously and colourfully peopled by cardinals, priests, great patrons, the delegations of different nations, beggars, spies, thieves, prostitutes, and painters and sculptors from all over Europe.

Often ill, maybe as an after-effect of being kicked by a horse or perhaps from malaria, Caravaggio lived in extremes of wealth and poverty, splendour and wretchedness. He was asked to paint still-lives, paintings of flowers or fruit, a genre generally looked down upon in those days because it was considered inferior to the painting of the human figure. So he invented his own variation, posing young people taken off the streets alongside baskets of fruit, chalices and glass objects.

At that time there were two factions among the power-brokers in Rome: the French one, innovative and progressive, was linked to the Franciscans, while the Spanish one, traditional and predictable, was associated with the Jesuits. The artist moved into the house of Cardinal Del Monte, ambassador of the Grand Duke of Tuscany, who had French connections. The friends and hangers-on who flocked to the Cardinal's house included artists, *donne oneste* (rich prostitutes, called 'honest' because they sat in the front row in church and gave generously to charity – the great prelates would keep these ladies for themselves and their guests), and young men who were readily available or had extraordinary voices and were known for obvious reasons as *castrati*. The Cardinal's circle was cultured, bohemian, gossipy and inquisitive; its members even indulged in the study of alchemy, officially banned by the Church.

It was in 1599, through Cardinal Del Monte, that Caravaggio obtained his first public commission: three great paintings representing the life of St Matthew for the Contarelli Chapel in the church of San Luigi dei Francesi. This was the beginning of his success in Rome. What marked him out from his contemporaries was that he rejected the traditional formulae for such subject matter and gave his paintings a powerful sense of contemporary realism. But it was his

use of light that proved most startling and innovative. It was as if the episodes from St Matthew's life took place in complete darkness and were revealed by the artist at their most dramatic moment through a sudden blaze of light that burned them on to the retina.

A child of his time, Caravaggio loved the taverns and brothels of Rome and often frequented the Piazza Navona, a meeting-point for thieves and vagabonds. He could be seen out and about with a young servant, or playing in the park with a small, ugly black dog. A mass of contradictions, the artist was grotesque, dirty, bad-tempered, generous and brilliant by turns and often ran into trouble with the law. In 1600 he was accused of beating up a companion and

ABOVE: The fountain of Neptune in the Piazza Navona, one of Rome's largest and most splendid Baroque squares. The long and narrow form of the square derives from its original use as a stadium under Emperor Domitian in AD 86.

a year later wounded a soldier. In 1603 he was thrown into prison, and was only released through the intercession of the French ambassador. In April 1604 he allegedly threw a plate of artichokes into a waiter's face and stones at a guard. The next year he was arrested for misusing a weapon, and then because of some problem with a woman he had to go into hiding. But in May 1606 things went too far: during a game of real tennis a furious argument broke out, which degenerated into a duel in which Caravaggio killed his antagonist.

From that moment, he lived on the run. He went first to Naples and then to Malta, where the Knights of the Order of St John commissioned what was to be his only signed work, *Salome and the Beheading of St John the Baptist*, for the Valletta Cathedral. For self-preservation he kept on the move, painting when he could with whatever materials were to hand. Syracuse, Messina, Palermo and then Naples again … In Naples he was attacked outside an inn and badly wounded. When he recovered, in July 1610, he sailed for Rome, but was arrested on the way and imprisoned for two days, mistaken for someone else. The ship had meanwhile set sail again and so he lost all his belongings, including his painting equipment. Humiliated but not defeated, Caravaggio tried to catch up with the ship, travelling overland, but only got as far as Porto Ercole where he remained, waiting for a pardon to come from Rome so that he could return. But he died there on the beach from pneumonia, not yet 39 years old. Three days after his death the papal pardon came through.

Quite aside from maverick individuals such as Caravaggio, and strong-minded governments such as Venice, over the centuries the Church did not always have an easy time dealing with the rulers of foreign states either. Napoleon Bonaparte was a case in point: after his victorious Italian campaign in the 1790s he took home with him numerous works of art and cultural treasures. The peace treaty he concluded with Pius VI contained this clause: 'The Pope will cede to the French Republic a hundred paintings, busts and statues that will be chosen by a specially appointed committee: these objects will include the bronze bust of Julius Brutus and the marble one of Marcus Brutus, both in the Capitol, and also 500 manuscripts indicated by the above-mentioned committee.'

Even today, while the Pope can rely for his upkeep on the Vatican state, he has a fund for his own personal expenses, the amount of which is secret. John XXIII was a heavy smoker, getting through more than a pack a day, and Pius XI was crazy about cars: he is said to have owned ten or more, some of which were gifts. One annual appointment involving one of modern Italy's most famous industries, is always respected. When the chairman of Ferrari met Pope Benedict XVI for the first time, he brought with him a cheque for a million euros from the sale of the Ferrari Enzo number 400, to be donated to charity. Strange as it may seem, Enzo Ferrari, the creator of the legendary 'red horse', did not like travelling: in the last 40 years of his life he never left Modena, his birthplace. 'Old people are like antique furniture,' he insisted. 'The less you move them, the longer they last.'

MUSIC, TRAGEDY AND GENIUS

Although the Renaissance produced more than its share of polymaths who excelled in numerous spheres of activity – Leonardo is perhaps the best-known example – the magnificence of Italian art, sculpture and architecture at this time can easily obscure the country's contribution to other art forms, such as music. A thread of human tragedy ties the interior of southern Italy to the Tyrrhenian coast: around the end of the sixteenth century Prince Carlo Gesualdo da Venosa who, stricken by remorse for a double murder, had retired to the castle of Gesualdo in Campania, not far from the Tyrrhenian Sea, received from Venosa, in the mountains near Potenza, the news of the accidental death of his only son and heir, Emanuele. It was the end of the line for this extra-ordinary amateur man who had displayed such virtuoso and originality that he was honoured and revered by the cultural world of his day.

The descendant of a great Norman family, Gesualdo is perhaps one of the most unsettling characters in the history of music. He excelled in polyphonic music, composing madrigals and sacred works. Ahead of his time, he was quite distinct in style from his contemporaries Marenzio and Monteverdi: in his tonalities and harmonies he created novel, daring imbalances. Giovanni Battista Doni, the seventeenth-century theoretician, whose name gave us 'doh' in the tonic sol-fa system of musical notation, was the first to call him a genius. Wagner was inspired by him, borrowing from Gesualdo in the 'Ride of the Valkyries' and in *Tristan und Isolde*. Stravinsky venerated him, evoking his harmonies in his ballet *The Firebird*.

Some people have attributed the visionary quality of his music to his desire to expiate the tragic act of violence that marred his life, an event that took place one October night in his house in Piazza San Domenico Maggiore in Naples. Gesualdo, born in 1561, was the second son in his family and his love of music manifested itself at a very young age. His early life was entirely taken up with singing and with playing the lute and harpsichord, but in 1584 his elder brother died and the duty of producing an heir fell to Carlo. A marriage was arranged with his cousin Donna Maria d'Avalos, following a dispensation from Pope Sixtus V because they were so closely related. Donna Maria, a beautiful and fascinating woman, was not yet 30 but had already been widowed twice; her first husband was said to have died as a result of his excessive sexual activity.

The desired heir, Don Emanuele, was soon conceived and Carlo quickly lost all interest in his wife, returning to his preferred interests of young men and music. However, one day Maria was at a ball where she met someone who *was* interested in her, the Duke of Andria. It was Carlo's uncle who betrayed them; he himself had often tried – but failed – to seduce Donna Maria. Carlo was told while out hunting that the relationship had become common knowledge. He returned home, surprised the guilty pair in bed and killed them both with an arquebus (a long-barrelled gun).

On account of his rank, Gesualdo could not be prosecuted. In any case, he had been driven to murder not so much by personal resentment as by the social conventions of the time, which made his revenge almost an obligatory act. None the less, once he had taken refuge in his impregnable castle, he fell prey to a mental sickness of a manic-depressive kind. As a penance he had all the surrounding woodland cut down, so that his shame could not be hidden. As he himself said: 'There is no witness so terrible, no accuser so implacable, as the conscience that lives in the breast of every man.'

Four years later he married again, taking as his wife Eleonora d'Este, cousin of the Duke of Ferrara, Alfonso d'Este II. The union was celebrated in many odes, sonnets and madrigals. When Eleonora became pregnant they stayed in Ferrara for about two years, but the musical academy would not give him the status he wished and so he decided to return to the castle of Gesualdo. It lost its grim, fortress-like appearance and became a beautiful home, hosting a splendid musical court in an attempt to emulate Ferrara. And in this peaceful setting the prince devoted himself completely to music, composing two more books of madrigals. Then in his search for spiritual peace and God's forgiveness he eventually abandoned the secular world of the madrigal and applied himself entirely to sacred music; he also had churches and convents built.

But Carlo Gesualdo still failed to become a good husband. He continued to suffer from manic depression, which manifested itself in displays of masochism and sadism. He began to torment his wife, beating her, ignoring her and showing off his lovers. Every time Eleonora left him he would plead with her to return, only to renew the violence. But perhaps that is the price of genius.

THE ANCIENT STONE DWELLINGS OF MATERA

If the south of Italy is shaped a little like a foot, Matera lies just inland from a very high instep, looking towards the Gulf of Taranto and the Greek islands. This is a bizarre and amazing place. A rocky promontory close to a deep canyon several kilometres long with a torrent at the bottom, surrounded by two broad valleys in the form of an amphitheatre, it has been inhabited since prehistoric times. Human beings lived here when they were simple hunter-gatherers and pastoralists, dwelling in villages enclosed by deep trenches dug in the ground. It has been suggested that these trenches divided the village into different social classes, but more probably they served to keep in the livestock and to separate the sacred area from the settlement.

The region round about has very little rainfall, so the inhabitants had to capture and preserve rainwater in roof-cisterns or bell-cisterns dug in the tufa stone. The roof-cisterns were used to channel into a well subsoil infiltrations and natural condensation from temperature differences. The drop-shaped bell-cisterns, thanks to an extended network of small channels and a number of intercommunicating systems that facilitated purification, were ideal for channelling

RIGHT AND OPPOSITE: In the biblical-looking town of Matera, the façades are built with blocks of stone taken from the mountain; once you step over the threshold you find yourself actually inside the mountain. The old town was branded a national disgrace by Italian politicians half a century ago as it still didn't have a sewage system or electricity, and about 30,000 residents were forcibly evicted. When I last visited Matera I discovered that it is now being revitalized, with the old dwellings being turned into fashionable homes, restaurants and hotels.

water into homes called *sassi* (stones), since they were carved out of the rock. The wells were shared – elements of social cohesion and survival. The most majestic one, known as the Long Diver, runs under the main square for over 50 metres and at a depth of 15 metres.

Matera is one of the few places in the world whose inhabitants can justifiably claim to be still living in the same houses as their ancient ancestors – although by the mid-twentieth century these dwellings had degenerated into disease-ridden slums, and only recently has the area been the subject of extensive regeneration and improvement, which has also turned it into a tourist attraction.

The first homes were created in the natural caves, interconnected with branching tunnels and built up on the outside with whatever material came to hand. The excavations created several storeys below ground, inclined at such an angle that the high summer sun never penetrated beyond the cave entrance, although in winter the low sun was able to reach right to the back of the cave, giving it light and warmth. Because the caves were situated one on top of the other the roof of a house is sometimes a street with chimney-pots sticking out of it, or the floor of another house!

The *civitas*, the ancient nucleus of the town, which was enclosed by walls until the sixteenth century, can be considered a natural fortress, a plateau surrounded by a sheer precipice. It is no accident that the thirteenth-century cathedral was built up here: it indicates the importance of the site with respect to the *sassi*, which were considered at the time as little more than a cluster of dwellings beyond the walls and used as a burial ground. Down the centuries, the houses in the southern

part have come to be used more and more frequently as cellars for the production and storing of wine. Visitors today usually see just the outer reaches of the *sassi*, where over 18,000 people live and there are over 50 churches; below is an inextricable tangle of tunnels spreading beneath the city, a testament to human ingenuity.

PUGLIA, LAND OF CASTLES AND HORSES

The region of Puglia, the 'heel' of Italy, which looks onto the southern Adriatic and the Ionian Sea, has always been a meeting point between East and West. In the Cathedral of Otranto, situated in its southernmost tip, a twelfth-century mosaic depicts the Tree of Life, full of symbols, myths and legends from all parts of the then known world, ranging from the Tower of Babel to King Arthur. Over the centuries the region has seen a continual traffic of travellers, pilgrims, merchants and conquering armies. Here different cultures, civilizations and faiths have met, conversed and sometimes fought: the Greeks settled here; the Roman legions made their way down the Appian Way to the port of Brundisium (Brindisi), from where their triremes sailed forth to conquer 'Mare Nostrum' from the Carthaginians; the Byzantines planted their banners

PREVIOUS PAGE: Countryside on the border of Puglia and Basilicata, north of Matera.
ABOVE: Trulli houses in Alberobello, east of Matera.

here, imposing the Orthodox religion, only to be ousted by the Normans, and then by the Swabians, the Angevins, the Aragonese and the Bourbons.

In 216 BC, on the heights of Cannae, the Carthaginian general Hannibal inflicted a heavy defeat on the Romans. He had brought his army, complete with elephants, from Africa, marching up through Spain and France, over the Alps and all the way down the Italian peninsula until he reached this piece of open land. The Romans, forced to take up their position with the sea behind them and the sun in their faces, suffered terrible loses: 25,000 killed and 10,000 taken prisoner. Hannibal became master of all southern Italy.

The coast of Puglia bristles with towers and ramparts, recalling the continual wars with Turks, Saracens and Dalmatian pirates. Inland lies the Puglia of fortresses, chief of which is the Castel del Monte, the most mysterious of the buildings commissioned by Frederick II of Swabia. On 29 January 1240 he signed an order specifying the construction materials for his castle: local white or pink limestone, white or veined marble, and coralline breccia. The result was a building that dominates the surrounding countryside and acts as the focal point of a vast system of communications.

ABOVE: The Castel del Monte, north-west of Matera, built according to esoteric principles, was chosen to decorate the Italian one euro-cent coin.

The Emperor may never have stayed here, but none the less the whole place evokes the complex symbolic universe connected with the power that he represented. An obsession with the number eight is evident throughout. The building is a monumental block of octagonal form, with an octagonal tower at each of its eight corners. Its two floors are each divided into eight trapezoidal rooms corresponding to each of the sides of the octagon, and the Throne Room is situated on the eastern side, 'oriented' towards the sun and towards Christ, like the apse of a cathedral, and in correspondence with the main façade, where the portcullis was operated. Frederick II was a man of culture who surrounded himself with musicians, poets, astrologers and wizards. He loved the liberal arts, mathematics and architecture, being especially interested in the astronomical and astrological concepts that were considered very important at that time. The octagon was the favourite form of the religious–military order known as the Knights Templar, and they may have had something to do with the origins of the castle.

Over the centuries the building underwent certain alterations, which blurred some of the astronomical and astrological characteristics that had gone into its making. For example, in the

LECCE: BAROQUE GLORIES AND A FLYING SAINT

IN 1880 FERDINAND GREGOROVIUS, a German writer and historian, described the architectural splendours of the town of Lecce, between Brindisi and Otranto, in his *Wanderjahre in Italien* (*Wanderings in Italy*):

Most of the cloisters and palaces of Lecce were built between the sixteenth and the seventeenth century. The material used in their construction is a limestone of a fine golden yellow, which is very easy to work and which the artists found to be an excellent material for the ornaments and decorations of the exterior walls of the buildings. Nowhere else have I ever seen such richly adorned façades. In its exaggeration and in its mannered style, and with the playfulness of southern fantasy, this art often falls into the baroque, and yet one cannot deny that these defects have given the city the uniform and typical mark of an age; so that the overall impression is of a harmonious whole. Lecce can be described as the Florence of the baroque age. For this artistic tendency there is nothing in Italy that can compare to it. And it must be said that here the baroque element, thanks to an ancient feeling for form that has never died away and with the influence of the bright sky of this happy land, achieves a certain level of idealism.

Around the time that these buildings were being erected, a boy named Giuseppe Maria Desa was born in 1603 near Lecce in what was then the Kingdom of Naples. As a child he fell seriously ill for a long time, but was miraculously cured. Another extraordinary thing about him was that he had the ability to levitate. This was regarded as a special gift from God, but at the same time made him suspect in the eyes of the Church.

As a child he fell seriously ill for a long time, but was miraculously cured. Often he would wander around aimlessly and have visions. He was very slow and distracted, unable to tell a story through to the end. The boy was hopeless at his books: he had two uncles in the Franciscan Order, but he himself was rejected on account of his ignorance. Finally his mother got him accepted as a servant at the monastery of the Conventual Franciscans. He somehow managed to become a deacon and then, amazingly, a priest: one day the bishop decided to promote everyone, and so Giuseppe was ordained without ever having to answer any questions. That is why he is considered the patron saint of students! He also, presumably because of the levitation, performs the same office for both pilots and air passengers.

Giuseppe would often talk to God while in a trance. Even when his confrères pricked him with pins or burned him with blazing coals in an attempt to wake him, he never noticed a thing. Frequently he would rise from the ground and remain hanging in the air; in church he would fly towards the altar or hover above it, still kneeling. Giuseppe also performed many miracles, curing the blind and the sick, and there was always a crowd asking him for help and advice; he converted many people.

When his confrères came to talk to him he would immediately read their thoughts, often far more accurately than they would have wished. One morning he entered church to say mass and announced that the Pope had died during the night; he made the same announcement on two other occasions, for the deaths of Urban VIII and Innocent X, and his confrères, fearing someone with such powers of precognition, denounced him to the ecclesiastical authorities. Giuseppe was summoned before the Inquisition. He was afraid, but St Anthony of Padua appeared to him and gave him encouragement. While under interrogation he entered a trance, rising and hovering in the air. And so he was sent to Rome. The General Minister of the Franciscan Order realized how humble and honest Giuseppe was, but the Inquisition tribunal was still suspicious and decided to keep a close watch on him, sending him from one isolated monastery to another. For the last ten years of his life he was kept in seclusion, unable to write or receive letters, as if in prison, while crowds of people continued to seek him out. Giuseppe celebrated mass for the last time in August 1663, a month before his death. So many people flocked to see him, to touch him and to cut a piece from his sacred habit, that eventually his confrères had to hide the body.

ABOVE: Santa Croce in the Piazza della Prefettura in Lecce.

interior courtyard the southern wall acts as a large gnomon. On 23 October, when the sun enters the sign of Scorpio, and on 20 April, when with the same declination it enters the sign of Taurus, the shadow of the gnomon touches the northern wall; and on 23 November, with the sun in Sagittarius, the shadow touches the circumference within which the castle is inscribed. On the line of the conjunctions, the two eastern and western towers lie in the direction of the rising and setting sun. The entrance gateway is said to be connected with the inclination of the lunar orbit, while the ratios between its lengths show that note has been taken of the criterion of the golden section and the figures related to it.

In the eighteenth century, in a world in which the horse remained the only means of transport on land, Goethe was greatly struck by the splendour of the equipage and mounts of the Neapolitan nobility; in his *Italian Journey* he wrote: 'My emotions had never before been aroused by a horse … I had never seen such beautiful horses.' The horse of the Murge, bred in the limestone hills of Puglia, is the only one that has come down to us as a pure thoroughbred, although in such small numbers that it is now at risk of extinction. In earlier times it was bred exclusively by the aristocracy, by great landowners and by Frederick II of Swabia, who may have begun the lineage. With the arrival of the Savoy dynasty, however, the Murgese was downgraded to the level of a draught horse and farm animal, and later, once mechanization took hold on farms, it was bred purely for its meat. But for centuries they were among the most famous horses in Europe.

In the ancient world, Alexander the Great had a high opinion of his Taranto cavalry; so did Hannibal, who stocked up with 4000 foals in Puglia. The inhabitants of Puglia were so defiant of Rome and so strong on horseback that Emperor Valentinian forbade them to use horses, on pain of death: in just one campaign of repression the Romans killed 7000 rebels.

Frederick II, whose favourite mount was a black stallion named Draco, was an expert breeder of horses. His animals were the finest of the age and were considered a strategic weapon; severe punishments were imposed on those who tried to export them from the kingdom. Despite their beauty, the Emperor was interested in their function rather than their aesthetic qualities: they were raised not on the soft green plains but on the dry, stony hills, which made their legs stronger.

In the fifteenth century it was the Republic of Venice that produced the best horses, which could be transported by sea and then used in battle; the horses were bred and trained at the city's farm, known as La Cavallerizza, which was situated in Le Murge. In the seventeenth century the court of Madrid acquired stallions from here and in the eighteenth century it was their fellow-Hapsburgs at the court of Vienna who became interested in them. Among their purchases were two horses named Napolitano and Conversano, from which descend the two most important lines of Lipizzaner horses, well known today to those who have seen the splendid performances by the white stallions of the Spanish Riding School in Vienna.

BELOW: The bishop's throne at Canosa di Puglia, north-west of Matera, is held up by elephants, possibly inspired by Hannibal's animals.

4

REACHING THE SOUTH

CRUMBLING GLAMOUR & WILD BEAUTY

*Campania – Naples & Capri; Sicily – Messina, Etna, Syracuse,
Noto, Agrigento, Segesta, Monreale & Palermo*

ABOVE: The notorious Bay of Naples, viewed from the Carthusian monastery of San Martino, with Vesuvius in the distance.
OPPOSITE: Sorrento, just south of Naples, by night.
PREVIOUS PAGE LEFT: Segesta, Sicily, one of the most perfect and well-preserved examples of Greek Doric architecture.
PREVIOUS PAGE RIGHT: Byzantine mosaics are scattered throughout Italy; they were created while much of Europe was in the Dark Ages.

Johann Wolfgang von Goethe, the great German dramatist, travelling in Italy in February 1787, came to Naples. This is how he described the emotion of seeing the famous bay where Mount Vesuvius looks out to the islands of Capri, Ischia and Procida.

In the afternoon, a fine even landscape opened up before us. Our route ran spaciously between fields of green corn that formed a deep rich carpet. In the fields are lines of poplars, which have been thinned out so that they can serve as supports for the vines. And thus the journey continued to Naples within a neat, delightfully gentle and well-kept landscape, passing by exceptionally tall and sturdy vines, whose curled shoots stretched from poplar to poplar forming a sort of net.

To our left stood Vesuvius with its heavy smokestack; and I rejoiced that I was finally seeing this extraordinary spectacle with my own eyes. The sky became brighter and brighter, and eventually the sun was beating down upon our carriage. As we got closer to Naples, the air became purer; by now we had moved into another land altogether. The flat roofs of the houses were an indication of a different climate; even if they cannot be very comfortable dwellings inside. Everyone was out in the streets, sitting and enjoying the sun while it lasted. The Neapolitan is convinced that he lives in paradise, and has a very poor opinion of the lands of the north: 'Always snow; wooden houses; great ignorance; but a lot of money.'

And, more recently, the story goes that a Milanese industrialist on a visit to Naples struck up the following conversation with a local man who was fishing.

'What are you doing?'

'I'm fishing – and enjoying the sun.'

The northerner felt it his duty to teach the local more about business practice. 'But if you organized yourself a bit better, you could catch more fish and make more money.'

'So?'

'Then you could buy a fishing boat, and really catch some fish.'

'And then?'

'Then? With the money you make you could buy a second boat,' the Milanese business-man insisted.

The Neapolitan seemed unconvinced.

'And you could put skippers in charge of your fleet, so you could go off and bask in the sun undisturbed.'

At this point the fisherman looked at him. 'Well, until you arrived, what was I doing?'

The Neapolitan mentality – in which living on your wits plays such a part – is perhaps exemplified by what happened when the wearing of seat-belts in cars became compulsory. On the day that the law came into force, cheap T-shirts with a seat-belt printed across the front were being sold on street stalls, and looking through car windows the police could barely tell the difference!

The streets are still bustling, and it was at one of the stalls in Piazza San Domenico near the Chapel of San Severo that – appropriately enough, given its reputation – I once bought a human skull. The thing was wrapped in newspaper, which came undone in the hands of a friend who wanted to know what I had bought. Her screams, when she saw what she was holding, were a perfect demonstration of another aspect of the Neapolitans: superstition. No one seems to be without their coral horn talisman, and index and little finger are often held out to form a pair of 'horns' that are supposed to ward off bad luck.

Horns, of course, are symbolic of other activities too. People claim that in southern Italy marital infidelity is a lethal affair. However, San Martino, a small town near Naples, hosts a Procession of Cuckolds every year on 11 November. The men gather in the main square wearing a set of bull or ibex horns, then they proceed to the church where the parish priest offers refreshments. The event ends with the burning of a puppet cuckold and the festive welcoming of new cuckolds to their ranks.

Of the various sanctuaries in the city, that of the Madonna dell'Arco – protector of thieves and whores – dates back to the mid-fifteenth century. The story goes that one Easter Monday a group of youths were playing a ball game called *palla a maglio* near an image of the Madonna and Child painted within the arch of an aqueduct. During the match, a ball bowled by one of the players was deflected by an old lime tree near the holy image and as a result he lost. In a fit of rage he cursed and hurled the ball away: it hit the Virgin's cheek, which then began to bleed. A nobleman who acted as the local *giustiziere* (judge) hauled the young man into court and summarily condemned him to be hanged – from the lime tree itself. Just two hours later, a dumbfounded crowd saw the dangling body wither.

On another Easter Monday, around a century later, a woman named Aurelia Del Prete came to the chapel carrying a piglet as an offering to the Madonna for curing her husband of a serious eye disease. However, as the woman made her way, with difficulty, through the crowds of the faithful the wriggling piglet slipped from her grasp. Trying but failing to grasp it once again, she kicked the piglet in exasperation and cursed the holy image in front of the church. Her horrified husband prophesied that the feet that had profaned the offering would now wither.

ABOVE AND OPPOSITE: The immortalized, ethereal beauty of the Resurrected Christ by Giuseppe Sammartino, a young sculptor who instilled his work with strong emotions. During a visit to Naples, Canova was so impressed by this sculpture that he asked if he could buy it.

RAIMONDO DI SANGRO, who was born in 1710, belonged to a family that boasted descent from Charlemagne, the founder of the Holy Roman Empire. His mother, Cecilia, died just one year after his birth and later – either due to grief or in reaction against his previous life of dissolution – the boy's father, Antonio di Sangro, shut himself away in a monastery. At the age of 20, Raimondo, having inherited the title of Prince of San Severo, returned to the family palazzo in Naples.

Two thousand years before, within the Egyptian quarter of the ancient Neapolis, this site had been occupied by a temple to Isis. Its walls ran with blood: at the end of the sixteenth century the then owner had killed his wife and her lover here, exposing their mutilated bodies on the balcony. Legend and rumour surrounded the new occupier, too. Raimondo, in many ways a perfect example of an Enlightenment aristocrat, had wide-ranging interests including weapons and military matters as well as literature, science and alchemy. He set up laboratories in his palazzo and was responsible for a number of inventions – an 'eternal light', which burnt yet consumed very little material (perhaps the result of a chemical

THE CHAPEL OF SAN SEVERO

mixture that included pulverized bone from a human skull); a waterproof cloak created for the Bourbon king Charles III; a rear-loading rifle, some 50 years ahead of its time; and a floating carriage that was used to cross the Bay of Naples.

More curious artefacts are to be found in the Sangro family chapel: in a statue of the Resurrected Christ the veil is so finely rendered that the figure appears to have been carved first and the marble veil added afterwards; the fall of light and shadow across the folds make this work much more an expression of poetry than one of pain and death. The same skill is to be seen in two other statues, allegories of Modesty and The Disabused. The former depicts a female nude draped with a very fine and extraordinarily realistic veil; the second a male figure who is being assisted by an angel to break free of a net, also rendered in perfect detail. These could be considered images of the prince's father and mother, whilst the Resurrected Christ may be Raimondo himself:

obsessed by questions of immortality and resurrection, the prince here tries to break through the veil of ignorance under the watchful eye of the parents he lost so early.

Others claim that the entire chapel was inspired by the rituals of the order of Freemasonry, to which Raimondo belonged. For example, the labyrinthine pattern on the floor – in black and white, the colours of good and evil – is said to be an allusion to the path of initiation. Similarly, the triangle surmounting the head of the white dove depicted on the ceiling could be taken as a symbol of both fire and the divinity. As for the three statues, these illustrate how, with the aid of reason, man can break through the veil of falsity. The most exceptional – and most gruesome – items are the so-called 'anatomical machines' in an annexe to the chapel: two flayed human bodies in which one can see the entire circulatory system down to the smallest capillary. As part of his quest to discover the elixir of life, it is thought that Raimondo injected a mysterious coagulant into the veins of two servants while they were still alive. Not surprisingly, Raimondo was excommunicated for his pains.

ABOVE: A wall painting from Pompeii, rescued from oblivion since careful and systematic excavations and reconstruction of the site began in the mid-eighteenth century. Work on uncovering the buried treasures continues today.
OPPOSITE: The Carthusian monastery of San Martino on the hill of Vomero. It was enlarged and radically redesigned in the 1600s.

True enough, Aurelia was struck down by a disease that confined her to bed, and a year to the day later her feet dropped off. They are still on public display as a warning to all those who take the name of God and his saints in vain.

The city inhabited by these superstitious folk was founded in 470 BC by Greek settlers, who named it Neapolis (New City) to distinguish it from the previous Palaepolis (Old City) that had been built centuries earlier on the site of the tomb of the mythological siren Parthenope. Attracted by the position and climate, the Romans subsequently conquered it, turning the area into a resort to which they could escape from life in the capital. Then, in AD 79, came the catastrophic eruption of Vesuvius, which buried the nearby cities of Pompeii and Herculaneum under 30 metres of boiling mud and lava.

Some saw the disaster as punishment for the lascivious lifestyle associated with these cities. Pompeii had become a city of pleasure: its women beautified themselves using wine must and red ochre to colour their cheeks, charcoal eyeliner and eye shadow made of pulverized malachite. Frescoes, sculptures and bas-reliefs adorning homes and inns as well as, more understandably, brothels were inspired predominantly by images of passion.

In the early Middle Ages, Naples became caught up in the power struggles between the invading Goths and the Byzantines – indeed, it would be tossed around like a plaything from one power to another, usually depending on who had won the latest war, for hundreds of years. After being the capital of an independent duchy for more than three centuries it came in the twelfth century under the rule of the Normans, and subsequently passed to the Hohenstaufens of Swabia. With the arrival of the Angevin French in the thirteenth century, who transferred their capital here from Palermo, the city underwent great expansion. Towards the end of that century a new fortress – Castel Nuovo, also known as the Maschio Angioino – was built.

In the late fourteenth century, Charles II of Anjou ('the Lame') was succeeded by his son Robert I ('the Wise'), who attracted to his court many outstanding cultural figures including the poet Petrarch, the Sienese painter Simone Martini and the artist Giotto, as well as commissioning the construction of the Carthusian monastery of San Martino on the hill of Vomero overlooking the city. Now a museum, this building includes among its exhibits a

collection of Neapolitan majolica and eighteenth-century Christmas nativity scenes; the elaborate terracotta figures are dressed in precious fabrics, exemplifying a traditional art that still flourishes in the city's Spanish Quarter – dating back to the mid-fifteenth century when the Angevin rulers were replaced by the Spanish house of Aragon.

For two centuries thereafter, Naples and Sicily were governed by Spanish vice-regents. My Neapolitan grandmother, Eugenia de Vito Piscicelli, is descended from one of the earliest of them, Don Pedro Alvarez de Toledo, who lived in the mid-sixteenth century. His significance is that he recalled the local barons and gentry from their feudal estates, thus initiating the construction of a large number of monumental *palazzi* within the city. The urban layout of Naples changed radically, and a major thoroughfare, the Via Toledo, opened up the city. These were times of great artistic originality and splendour in Naples, as witnessed by the Royal Palace and various Baroque churches. But for ordinary Neapolitans life under the despotic vice-regents, who imposed punitive taxes, was harsh and this resulted in riots and rebellions. In the early eighteenth century there was further suffering when a terrible outbreak of plague killed some 400,000 citizens. Things took a turn for the better when the Spanish returned, after a brief Austrian interlude, in the person of Charles of Bourbon, under whom Naples became once more the capital of an independent state, the Kingdom of the Two Sicilies. The territory reflected the form of the ancient Greek Magna Graccia, which had extended along the coast of southern Italy from the Gulf of Taranto to the Strait of Messina and northwards as far as Volturno in Campania.

Charles, only 17 when he ascended the throne, was receptive to guidance and good advice and dedicated himself to wide-ranging reforms in the fields of trade, economics, fiscal policy and the administration of justice. He also re-established diplomatic relations with other states, including the Holy See. On the eve of St Peter's Day feudal vassals to the Church, including the kings of Naples and Sicily, traditionally presented the Pope with the gift of a white thoroughbred horse with a silver coin-filled urn strapped to the saddle. The animal was brought into the Vatican, where it would bend its knee before the pontiff. Charles's other great achievement was the building of a majestic new palace a little inland at Caserta, designed by the architect Vanvitelli and linked to Naples by a grandiose avenue. With its modern urban layout, this city-court became the very heart of the kingdom. In terms of magnificence, scale and monumentality it was the Bourbons' answer to Versailles.

The Bourbons remained monarchs of Naples practically up to the unification of Italy. There were only two interruptions: in 1799, when a Repubblica Partenopea, inspired by the principles of the French Revolution, was founded; and during the period of Napoleonic rule, from 1806 to 1815. It was King Ferdinand IV of Naples who bestowed upon Horatio Nelson, admiral of the British fleet, the Duchy of Bronte in Sicily as a reward for services rendered. Nelson's descendants still live there.

OPPOSITE: The Grand Staircase in the Royal Palace of Naples. Begun in the early 1600s, it was extensively remodelled in the neo-classical style for Gioacchino Murat and Carolina Bonaparte, then again, following a fire, in 1837. There is now a public library in the royal apartments.

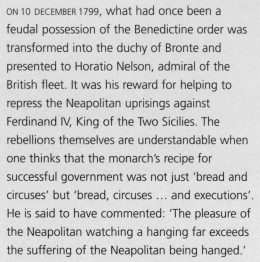

ON 10 DECEMBER 1799, what had once been a feudal possession of the Benedictine order was transformed into the duchy of Bronte and presented to Horatio Nelson, admiral of the British fleet. It was his reward for helping to repress the Neapolitan uprisings against Ferdinand IV, King of the Two Sicilies. The rebellions themselves are understandable when one thinks that the monarch's recipe for successful government was not just 'bread and circuses' but 'bread, circuses … and executions'. He is said to have commented: 'The pleasure of the Neapolitan watching a hanging far exceeds the suffering of the Neapolitan being hanged.'

Before he left Naples for Egypt, to surprise the French fleet in Aboukir Bay near Alexandria and triumph at the battle of the Nile, Nelson had been dazzled by the beauty of Emma Hamilton. Born in Wales in 1763, she came from very humble origins. Her mother took her to London when she was 14 and set her to work first as a fruit-seller, then as a chambermaid. Always upwardly mobile, while working in an inn Emma began the first of a series of affairs that would culminate in her most famous relationship, with Nelson. Living at a country house, Uppark, with another lover she next made the acquaintance of society painters such as George Romney and Thomas Lawrence and of noblemen such as Charles Greville, whose mistress she became when her previous *amour* lost his fortune. Now a dazzling society figure, during this period she

BRITISH ADMIRAL, SICILIAN DUKE

met Greville's uncle, William Hamilton, English ambassador to Naples, who fell in love with her.

When Greville duly succumbed to financial ruin, he decided the only way out was to disentangle himself from his mistress and marry a rich woman. He therefore asked Emma to move with his uncle to Naples, where she swiftly reprised her role as a great hostess. Goethe's *Italian Journey* records: 'Sir William Hamilton, who resides here as the English ambassador, has – after spending a long period as a passionate lover of the Arts and an eager student of Nature – now found the greatest joys of Art and Nature combined in a beautiful girl: a very attractive and comely young English woman of around twenty years old whom he keeps at his house … '

As time passed, Emma and Hamilton became closer and she was even accepted at court by King Ferdinand and Queen Mary Caroline, sister of the ill-fated Marie-Antoinette. The couple married in England on 6 September 1791. On their way back to Naples they stopped in Paris at a time when King Louis XVI and Marie-Antoinette were already virtually prisoners of the Revolutionary authorities in the Tuileries palace. Emma, however, managed to convey a message from the French queen to her sister.

Once back in Naples, she then met the man with whom her name is most closely associated: Lord Nelson. Even though Revolutionary France was popular with various levels of Neapolitan society, Emma – who often intervened in politics – managed to obtain the support that Nelson needed to facilitate his victory over the French fleet. In September 1798 the returning hero – his face swollen and badly scarred – was met by a fleet decked out with flowers and hung with Neapolitan and English flags. Under the command of Francesco Caracciolo (an ancestor of my Neapolitan grandmother), the welcoming ships carried the royal family, Sir William Hamilton and the woman whom the nineteenth-century French writer Alexandre Dumas described as 'that English Circe, whose words would soon captivate the victor of Aboukir, a man less prudent than Ulysses'.

King Ferdinand hailed Nelson as his liberator and protector and decorated him with the Grand Cross of the Order of St Ferdinand, as well as making him Duke of Bronte. From Queen Caroline, Nelson received a ring bearing the inscription 'To the hero of the Nile'. And Lady Hamilton rewarded him with the most fateful – and precious – gift of all: her love. The admiral stayed at the Hamiltons' residence, where Emma's treatment of his wounds with ass's milk proved so successful that he was well enough to attend a massive ball with almost 2000 guests that was given to celebrate his birthday that same month.

Gifts and honours were showered on him from all over Europe (bar France, naturally enough), but for the moment Nelson had put naval derring-do behind him and became an infatuated lover. He wrote to his poor wife Fanny in London, confessing that he really ought to leave Naples while also trying to fool himself into thinking that his presence there was essential to the royal family and to Britain's political interests. After all, wasn't it the admiral and his fleet who provided the support for the Neapolitan monarchy promised by London? Throughout this period Nelson may have felt some remorse for his conduct, but he no longer listened to reason; his passion for Lady Hamilton was overwhelming.

By the turn of the century Napoleon had established various republics in central and northern Italy, swearing undying enmity to the Bourbons in the south; he even went so far as to describe Mary Caroline as a lesbian. The queen responded that to the likes of Bonaparte one did *not* respond: she was the daughter of the Empress of Austria, he a mere *bourgeois*. But her own people, too, whispered about the queen's various lovers, hinting at a relationship with Emma Hamilton herself.

The war against Napoleon continued. Soon French forces reached Naples, where a rebellion headed by enlightened members of the aristocracy and the bourgeoisie resulted in the foundation of the Repubblica Partenopea. The king and queen managed to escape to Palermo thanks to help from Lord Nelson, who also assisted William and Emma Hamilton to get away to England.

The leading figures in the new republic included Francesco Caracciolo, who had sailed out to meet the triumphant Nelson. They eventually thrashed out a new constitution, based on that adopted by France in 1795, as well as tackling

the issues of public education and agrarian reform. However, the length of time taken to repeal feudal laws frustrated the peasantry, with the result that Mary Caroline – Ferdinando IV had meanwhile died in Palermo – and Cardinal Fabrizio Ruffo formed local brigands and peasants into what became known as the Army of the Holy Faith. They managed to penetrate Naples, where they defeated the Republicans, unleashing a period of violent repression in which many were condemned to death. Mary Caroline – together with Emma Hamilton – often watched the executions, one of whose victims was Francesco Caracciolo.

Thus the Bourbons returned to Naples, and in the early years of the 1800s Emma bore Nelson a daughter, Horatia, to whom he was devoted. Their respective spouses seemed to accept the situation, but the same cannot be said of English society. In April 1803 William Hamilton died, and his estate was inherited by his nephew Greville. Emma, who received just £100, went to live at the house of Nelson's brother, William. The battle of Trafalgar in

October 1805 was an overwhelming British victory: the French fleet was almost entirely destroyed, Napoleon humbled, and Britain's position as Queen of the Seas confirmed. However, at the age of 47 Nelson was dead, the fatal shot fired by a French sniper who had spotted the admiral standing on the bridge of his ship.

He was buried with full honours in Westminster Abbey; but his brother did not respect the clauses in his will that concerned Emma Hamilton. Left in penury, she wrote to Queen Mary Caroline begging for help; but her former friend did not deign to reply. Twice imprisoned for debt, Emma Hamilton died a pauper in Calais in 1815, aged 52.

OPPOSITE LEFT: Ferdinand IV of Naples.
OPPOSITE RIGHT: Admiral Horatio Nelson, sketched in Naples in 1797.
ABOVE: Naples and the Castel Nuovo at the time of Nelson's presentation.

Under Bourbon rule the city underwent extensive transformation and modernization, the new public buildings – such as the first Teatro San Carlo and the Capodimonte Palace, famous for its porcelain – being intended to rival those in the other capitals of Europe. Naples was also home to the first railway line in Italy, running between the city and the town of Portici; steam locomotives continued to be used for decades, even after the introduction of electricity and diesel. And just one year after the opening of the railway line, two entire districts of Naples were illuminated by gas-lit street lamps.

The dream of a unified Italy had, however, conquered the popular imagination, and there was overwhelming enthusiasm when Garibaldi arrived in 1860, marking the annexation of the city by the Kingdom of Savoy. But when Rome, too, became part of the new nation in 1870, that city also came to dominate its cultural identity. Rather than being absorbed within the modern Italy, the identity of the ancient Magna Graecia became what we might call a 'sub-identity', shared by all the peoples of the South.

Naples has none the less retained all its own special vivacity, a quality that was convincingly captured by the writer and architect known by the pseudonym Curzio Malaparte, who built a villa on the island of Capri, whose name translates as 'Home like Myself'. Capri has been famed for its beauty since classical times. Later Oscar Wilde and Lenin, among others, sought refuge here, and in the 1950s and 1960s it attracted the jet set: Brigitte Bardot; Humphrey Bogart; Tina Onassis, daughter of the Greek shipping magnate; Maria Callas, one of his wives; the last Shah of Persia and his first wife, Soraya; Ingrid Bergman and Roberto Rossellini; Rita Hayworth and her husband, the Aga Khan. Then, of course, there was Malaparte, who lived out a narcissistic quest for eternal youth in his bizarre clifftop villa. The crescent-shaped walls that enclose the roof terrace – approached by stairs on either side of the building – were constructed so that Malaparte would be safe from prying eyes when, stark naked, he launched into his work-out sessions. Meanwhile, the writer went through a variety of political creeds from Republicanism to Fascism, and then from Anti-Fascism to Communism. Finally, without abandoning any of his previous irony or cynicism, he turned to Catholicism and was shamelessly inclined to weep and pray!

In Malaparte's novel *La Pelle* (*Skin*), set in post-war Naples, the street crime is always accompanied by a touch of humour. One character, for example, goes around carrying a rucksack with a small child inside; every time they pass a man wearing a cap, the child shoots out, snatches it and then – quick as a flash – disappears back into the rucksack. That sums up Naples and the south of Italy, its street life and festivities dating back to time immemorial. Some traditions have a very practical origin, often associated with a fundamental resource that can be very scarce in this part of Italy: water. In Salerno, the tradition continues of diverting the river every summer so that its waters slowly flow through the town itself. And in the Catanzaro area there is an old story that, during a particularly severe drought, the inhabitants threatened

BELOW AND OPPOSITE: Two views of the Strait of Messina, the intimidating waters between eastern Sicily and southern Calabria. The natural whirlpool causes confusion in the currents and probably gave rise to the legends of Scylla and Charybdis.

their patron saint that his statue could end up in the river: 'Either you get us wet, or we'll get you wet.' And according to legend, it duly rained. Vivacity seems to flow in these people's veins – along with a dash of originality: near Cosenza, for example, the mayor of a small town got so fed up with the vandalism of gangs of youths that he challenged the culprits to a duel – to be fought, with real weapons, in the town square.

BEYOND THE STRAIT: THE FIRES OF ETNA

Off the mainland lies Sicily, an island of Magna Graecia colonized in the eighth century BC by the Greeks, occupied in the fifth by the Carthaginians and then in 241 BC by Rome, which made the island its first province. After the fall of the Empire, Sicily was ruled successively by the Ostrogoths, the Phoenicians, the Byzantines, the Arabs, and then a host of other foreign rulers.

Sailing across the Strait of Messina is a hazardous enterprise even today; we can see why the ancients saw such a crossing as a venture into the unknown, a confrontation with hostile elements and with chaos represented by the forces of nature. The old Greek myths can still surprise us with their evocative power.

On a rock in the strait lived a legendary monstrous creature known as Charybdis, daughter of the Earth and of Poseidon. Three times every day Charybdis swallowed up the sea-water with all that it contained, including ships, and then vomited it all out again. When Ulysses crossed the strait for the first time he eluded the monster but, after being wrecked as a punishment for sacrilege, he was drawn in by the current of Charybdis. However, he was clever enough to cling to a fig tree that grew at the entrance of the cave where the monster lay hidden and when she spewed out the ship's mast Ulysses was able to grab hold of it and survive to continue his journey.

OPPOSITE: The essence of Sicily – Mount Etna, limpid waters, fragrant vegetation and prickly pears. Until the Romans started planting fields of grain, the whole island was one great forest.

Within a bowshot of Charybdis, towards the opposite shore of the strait, another monster awaited all voyagers. This was Scylla, hidden in the depths of a cavern in a rock inaccessible to mortals. In the *Odyssey* Homer recounts how Glaucus, who was in love with Scylla, the daughter of a god, rejected the love of the sorceress Circe. In order to avenge herself on her rival, Circe mixed together noxious herbs in the water of the spring where Scylla bathed. The young woman's body was transformed: six monstrous hounds bursting from her waist devoured everything within reach.

Schinkel, a nineteenth-century German architect and court painter, described the Strait of Messina in these terms: 'The coast of Calabria is grand and terrible, the Sicilian shore is more gentle and welcoming even up to the peak of Etna, with its milder nature.' Presumably he had never been there at the time of an eruption. Etna, the largest of the volcanoes in southern Italy, looms immense, a fateful presence that has marked the history of the people and places in its shadow. It is never dormant; with over 100 recorded eruptions, from time to time it emits enormous puffs of smoke that turn to gigantic smoke rings as they rise. The Latin poet Virgil described the mountain in dramatic words: 'Etna roars with awful rumblings. Sometimes, it spews forth a dark cloud into the air, with black whirling smoke and burning ashes, and it throws up balls of fire so high that they seem to touch the stars! Sometimes, it hurls forth boulders, torn from the bowels of the mountain, moaning and casting forth liquefied rocks from the boiling depths of its heart.'

The volcano was probably formed at the bottom of the sea, and emerged from the waves as magma (molten rock) accumulated about half a million years ago. The ancients talked of it as the forge of Vulcan and Cyclops, or as the pillar of heaven, under which lay the giant Enceladus or Typhon, who shakes the earth as he writhes.

One of the most significant eruptions of ancient times occurred in 396 BC, when the lava flowed as far as the sea. In the Middle Ages an eruption formed new craters from which gushed three streams of lava, two of which again poured into the sea. The worst eruption of relatively modern times was in 1669. Preceded by local earthquakes, an immense torrent of lava came pouring out, destroyed part of the city of Catania and flowed out into the sea for a distance of 6 or 7 kilometres. Very recently, in 1998, a series of seismic quakes was accompanied by activity in the craters at the summit, after which a huge explosion reopened the central crater and sent out a thick cloud of ash that swathed the whole of Catania.

Etna may be the most powerful of the volcanoes hereabouts, but of course it is not the only one. Set within the curve of the coast that marks the boundary between the zone of the Tyrrhenian Sea that sank during the Middle Tertiary period, when the Apennines came into being, and the raised zone on which Italy's volcanoes are situated, the Aeolian islands are all of volcanic origin, rising from a marine depth of about 2000 metres. Two of the islands have given their names to specific forms of volcanic activity. The term 'Vulcanian' refers to the kind of

activity that takes place when a plug is blown violently from a crater, releasing cinders and a dark cloud full of ash. 'Strombolian' activity is marked by explosions of moderate intensity at short intervals that throw up a thick, incandescent lava; this lava, accompanied by a white cloud of ash-free steam, tends to solidify on the surface while the trapped gases are periodically emitted, provoking explosions.

Vulcano, known to the Greeks as Hierà, meaning 'sacred', and thought to be the ancient island of Hephaestos, the Greek god of fire, is now uninhabited on account of its ceaseless volcanic, smoky emissions all over the island. The last great eruption took place in 1888 and forced the few settlers on the island to abandon their work of extracting sulphur and alum, an industry that had begun under the dynamic leadership of a Scotsman, James Stevenson, who came here in 1870. The ancient inhabitants used to bury their dead close to the volcano, considering it a link between the world of the living and that of the dead.

Stromboli is the only island in the archipelago with permanent volcanic activity. Its dark conical shape and the flickering glow of its volcano at night were recognized by the earliest navigators who ventured into the Tyrrhenian.

The isle of Salina was called Didyme by the first colonizers from ancient Greece, on account of the 'twin' peaks that tower over the sea. In the valley between them are vineyards, where Malvasia grapes are grown to make the wine known for centuries in England as Malmsey. The last volcanic eruption is said to have taken place about 13,000 years ago; today the only activity consists of underwater emissions of pungent hydrogen sulphide, known by the locals as *sconcassi* or commotions. And volcanoes are not always bad news: in ancient times the inhabitants of the island of Lipari grew rich on the export trade in black obsidian.

In the summer of 1831, on the southern coast of Sicily, there was a series of earth tremors: the water seethed and columns of smoke hung over the sea. And then an island arose from the waves, over 50 metres in height. The island, which was named Ferdinandea after Ferdinand of Bourbon, remained there only five months before being engulfed by the waves again. In that brief space it was visited by many sightseers from Italy and abroad, including two Englishmen; despite the heat emanating from the eruptive material, in which their feet sank up to the ankles as they walked, this phlegmatic pair calmly sat down and had lunch.

EARTHQUAKES AND REBUILDING

The first city across the strait, where one day a bridge may be built, is Messina. Here too people sit calmly on the harbour-side, eating, watching the ferries or fishing, oblivious to the tumultuous history and physical instability of the 'island of fire'. The strait and its waters have their tragic myths, and the land that looks onto them has no shortage of terrible stories either. On the night of 28–29 December 1908 a great roar was heard and the land shook. At the Ximenian

Observatory in Tuscany they noted: 'This morning at 5.21 the instruments of the Observatory registered a staggering, extraordinary movement: the tracings were so wide that they did not fit inside the cylinders: they measure over 40 centimetres.' The earthquake reached 10 on the Mercalli scale, and 90 per cent of the buildings of Messina were destroyed.

Some survivors remained close to their homes, while others decided it would be safer to head towards the sea. But among the yawning chasms and heaps of rubble many of the former became victims of gas explosions and of the fires that broke out. Those who had gone to the harbour were no safer: the water was suddenly sucked back and three great tidal waves, over 10 metres high, came crashing onto the shore, smashing whatever was left. As the sea receded again it dragged with it boats, corpses, the wounded and the survivors. In Messina alone there were 80,000 victims, more than half its population. The mainland was affected, too. In the province of Reggio Calabria 15,000 people were killed out of a population of 45,000. It was one of the worst catastrophes in Italian history, an economic disaster from which the region has never recovered; even now, a century later, a small portion of our taxes are still reserved for Messina.

The Minister for the Navy ordered Italian ships sailing in Sardinian waters to turn about and head for the disaster zone. But by the morning of 29 December a number of other ships had already reached Messina: a Russian naval squadron that was anchored nearby, as well as some British warships, offered aid to the Sicilians and Calabrians. Meanwhile, King Victor Emmanuel III decreed that a special medal of merit should be struck, in two sizes and with three orders; the larger format was to be awarded to deserving organizations, and the smaller to private individuals. On a more practical note, it was nearly 30 years before the 'temporary' huts for the homeless were replaced by proper buildings!

Such catastrophes were not new in the course of Messina's long history. Its population had frequently been almost wiped out by epidemics, and the earthquake of 1783, during the Bourbon rule of Ferdinand IV, had destroyed most of the city. After its reconstruction, it suffered severe bomb damage during the nineteenth-century Risorgimento period, a time of nationalism and revolution, when it was shelled by the Bourbon forces.

Noto, on the southern tip of Sicily, was razed by an earlier earthquake in 1693. It was rebuilt during the eighteenth century on another hill, closer to the coast. The new city is a masterpiece of Baroque town planning, unique for its size and homogeneity, achieving a marvellous visual balance between the solid structures of the palaces and churches and the open spaces of the squares and streets, and perfect harmony between materials and styles. The central square is a Baroque jewel, dominated by the broad flight of steps leading up to the theatrical façade of the cathedral. The interior was, unfortunately, half-destroyed in 1996 when the dome collapsed. Reconstruction commenced in 1999. The streets – like those in other towns on the island – are often traversed by characteristic colourful Sicilian carts that have changed little for hundreds of years.

REACHING THE SOUTH

RIGHT: Wonderful Sicilian carts like
this one were used for the everyday
transportation of goods and people.
The scenes painted on the sides
were inspired by the fanciful tales
of battles, kings, ladies, chivalry
and the gallant deeds of the
paladins of France.

OPPOSITE: One of six extraordinary
sculpted stone balconies that adorn
the Palazzo Villadorata in Noto.

THE GREEK HERITAGE

The first settlement in Noto was founded by the citizens of nearby Syracuse in the eighth century BC. It flourished under Greek dominion in the second century BC, with its sanctuary devoted to the goddess of the harvest, Demeter, its circle of city walls and sacred area, its agora (public open space) and theatre, remains of which can still be seen.

Taormina, just north of Noto, also had a long period of Greek influence, and the remarkable theatre from those times continues to bear witness to that presence. In the eighth century BC the Greeks, prevented from expanding eastwards by the powerful empires of Asia Minor, looked west and were attracted to rich and fertile Sicily. Groups of immigrants from the island of Naxos in the Aegean gave the name of their old homeland to their new settlement. After the conquest of Naxos in 403 BC Dionysius the Elder, the powerful 'tyrant' (ruler) of Syracuse, besieged the hill on which the acropolis then stood and where the Greek theatre was later built. On a night without moonlight, while a blizzard raged, his soldiers climbed

the crags and managed to take possession of the hill. The city was refounded under the name of Tauromenion by Greek refugees in 358 BC.

Early Greek colonization was confined to seaboard areas, but with the expansionist Dionysius it spread throughout Sicily. He ruled with intelligence, determination and cruelty, so that his city-state became one of the most powerful of the age, defending the identity of the Greek people against Carthaginians, Etruscans and Italiots (the resident population that pre-dated the Greeks), never hesitating to destroy other cities and founding colonies along the Adriatic as well.

His military and civil engineering enterprises required the collaboration of scientists and technicians; for example, the castle of Euryalus, built as a defence against the Carthaginians, had two ditches cut through the rock and towers overlooking the sea, or the Altar of Hieron, at 198 metres long the largest in the world, on which 540 oxen could be sacrificed together. Finally there was the Greek theatre, which later became a Roman amphitheatre, second only to the Arena in Verona, a setting for bloody gladiatorial fights. This fine example of the genre

was for centuries the hub of city life, and is still used today for the performance of Greek tragedies.

Traces of Greek civilization, from the sixth century BC up to the period of Dionysius, can be found throughout this island. Enemy captives were used to build these impressive works and excavate the stone from quarries known as *latomies*. The excellent acoustics in the cave in which the prisoners were housed enabled Dionysius to eavesdrop on them through a hole in the rock. Many centuries later, the painter Caravaggio, on the run from a death sentence for murder, visited the cave in 1608 and named it the Ear of Dionysius because of its shape and function. Accounts have come down to us of dialogues – at times pungent ones – between the tyrant and such philosophers as Plato, Diogenes the Cynic and Aristippus, who wrote the *Sentence for Dionysius* and the essay *On the Daughter of Dionysius*.

The close association between power and wisdom could be a little edgy, even though both sides derived advantage from it. Dionysius once asked Aristippus why philosophers went to the homes of the rich but the rich never went to those of philosophers, and he replied: 'Because the former know what they need, while the latter don't.' Another time, when the tyrant teased him by asking why he had come to him, he answered: 'When I needed knowledge, I went to Socrates; now that I need money, I come to you.' Diogenes often had a sharp word for the tyrant; when asked how Dionysius treated his friends, he said: 'He treats them like sacks: he hangs them if they're full, he throws them away if they're empty.' And when he was criticized for accepting money from Dionysius, while Plato had taken a book, he answered: 'I needed money, Plato books.'

After Dionysius, the island was taken over by the Carthaginians from North Africa. Then an even greater danger menaced Sicily: the Romans, who acquired the island during the first Punic War (against Carthage) in 246 BC, through whom Hieron II had tried to unify Greek Sicily. After his death the Romans fought another war against Carthage, which led in 212 BC to the destruction of Syracuse by the Roman legions. The citizens were massacred, among them the great scientist Archimedes. Following the Romans, who reconstructed many of the Greek buildings and added numerous new ones of their own, Taormina enjoyed a period of splendour under Byzantine rule. This was followed by Arab, Norman and Spanish rule, all of which contributed to the island's rich cultural tapestry.

Along a ridge further south, looking towards Africa, during the fifth century BC a considerable number of splendid Doric temples were built, which testify to the prosperity of the city of Agrigento. All the buildings face east, in accordance with the Greek and Roman belief that the entrance to the cell containing the god's statue must be lit by the rising sun, the source and guiding principle of life. The temples all have six columns on their façades with the exception of that to Zeus, with seven half-columns built into a wall that sealed the whole temple. This building – unfinished and now ruined, but still quite clearly huge – was erected around 480 BC in gratitude to the god after the Agrigentines' victory over the Carthaginians. It was one of the largest temples of ancient times, over 100 metres long and 50 wide. Some of the blocks still bear marks formed when they were raised: deep U-shaped grooves show where ropes, linked to a kind of crane, were threaded. The vast altar was used for important sacrifices: as many as 100 oxen could meet their end simultaneously. But the image that is always associated with Agrigento is the Temple of the Dioscuri. Built in the last decades of the fifth century BC, it is dedicated to the twins Castor and Pollux, born from the union of Leda and Zeus, the latter in the guise of a swan. It was here that the feast in honour of Demeter was celebrated by married women. All that is left now are four columns and part of the entablature. Some way off lie the few remains of the Temple of Hephaestos or Vulcan. According to legend the god of fire had his furnace under Etna, where he forged the thunderbolts of Zeus with the help of the Cyclops.

OPPOSITE: The Greek Temple of Heracles (Hercules) in the Valley of the Temples at Agrigento. The surviving monuments of the ancient city stand out as symbols of eternity, surrounded by the modern urban sprawl.

ARCHIMEDES OF SYRACUSE

ALTHOUGH ARCHIMEDES HAD NO OFFICIAL POSITION in the Second Punic War, he put his skills at the state's disposal in order to defend his city. His war-engines included a great catapult and, reputedly, a system of mirrors that concentrated the rays of the sun onto the invaders' ships and set them on fire. The order was given to capture Archimedes alive: he was well known in Rome for his extraordinary skills as an inventor, and nobody wanted such a genius to be one of the victims in the war against Carthage. However, things didn't go quite as planned – it seems that a soldier entered Archimedes' house, asked him who he was and then ordered the old man to follow him; absorbed in his calculations, the mathematician took no notice and the soldier ran him through with his sword.

Archimedes had studied at Alexandria in Egypt, perhaps as a pupil of Euclid, and then spent most of his life in Sicily, devoting himself wholly to research. He was one of the greatest mathematicians of antiquity, a brilliant inventor and a scholar of physics, optics, astronomy and geometry; his contributions to the study of the areas and volumes of flat and solid figures anticipated many of the findings of modern geometry – for example, the area of spherical surfaces. He gave a clear explanation of the principle of the lever, and in the field of hydro-statics he formulated the famous principle that is named after him: any body completely or partially submerged in a fluid is acted upon by an upward force that is equal to the weight of the fluid displaced by the body.

Legend has it that Hieron II wanted to offer a precious crown to the temple and had given a craftsman a lump of gold from which to create it. He now suspected that the goldsmith had adulterated the gold with silver, creating an alloy that still looked perfect to the eye. Not being able to prove this, he asked Archimedes to determine whether the crown was indeed made of pure gold.

Archimedes began to think intensely about the problem. As he stepped into his bath he noticed that the amount of water that flowed out of the tub was equal to the volume of the body that was entering. He immediately saw how he could ascertain the purity of the gold in the crown: he would prepare two blocks, one of gold and one of silver, of equal weight to the crown. He would put them both into water and measure the volume displaced by each. Then he would be able to see whether the crown had displaced a volume of water equal to the volume displaced by the block of gold; if it didn't, it would mean that the gold in the crown had been adulterated.

The story goes that in his enthusiasm he leaped out of the tub and ran through the house naked, shouting 'Eureka!' ('I've found it'). Apparently the goldsmith had indeed committed a forgery; one can only imagine what happened to the poor man. Sicilians still identify with Archimedes; at school my mother was known as 'little Archimedes' because she was very good at maths!

PIRANDELLO AND THE ABSURDITY OF LIFE

THE PROSPERITY AND CONFIDENCE of classical Agrigento were not shared by a more recent inhabitant who revolutionized drama and was one of the first writers to explore the subconscious mind. Born in 1867, Luigi Pirandello articulated the anxieties and doubts that trouble modern man, unable to grasp the concept that truth is relative and reality exists in multiple forms according to the perception of the individual. This he did even before 1916 when Albert Einstein published similar ideas from a scientific viewpoint in his theory of relativity.

Pirandello's description of his own life was the 'involuntary sojourn on earth' of a 'son of chaos' – his birthplace, the villa of his wealthy sulphur mine-owning family, was known as Chaos. The traumatic events of that life – financial ruin when one of the mines flooded, and the subsequent nervous collapse of his wife into a state of incurable paranoia – led Pirandello to explore, through his writing, the impenetrable nature of the human personality.

His first success came in 1904 with his third, and probably his best, novel – *The Late Mattia Pascal*, remarkable for the brilliance of its psychological observation. The main character lives a humdrum existence in a backwater town, then wins a lot of money and is able to experience a different kind of life away from his roots. Learning that back home he is rumoured to have committed suicide, he adopts a different persona. But his undefined social status makes his new existence an impossibility, so he fakes the suicide of his assumed persona. Returning home, he finds his wife has remarried and no one remembers him. As a result he has to retire into the background as a nonentity, for in the world's eyes he will always be 'the late Mattia Pascal'. Pirandello's character in this novel testifies perfectly to the absurd condition of man today, imprisoned by social conventions and duties, against which the desire to live life struggles in vain.

Pirandello then turned to the theatre, achieving international success with, in particular, his plays *Six Characters in Search of an Author* and *Henry IV*, both written in the 1920s. The former takes art, the latter madness, and contrasts them with what is perceived as 'normal' life. Pirandello had by now left Sicily for good; but his writing drew, paradoxically and increasingly, on his Sicilian background, expressing a view of life seen always in terms of tragic conflict. In 1934, two years before his death, he was awarded the Nobel Prize for Literature.

Along the roads, the deep ruts left by the builders' cart-wheels can still be seen; their extreme depth is perhaps due to the fact that they were later used as water-pipes. Between the Temple of the Dioscuri and the Temple of Hephaestos is the hollow of the 'garden of Kolymbetra', described by the historian Diodorus Siculus as the 'pool', a fine example of hydraulic engineering.

Built in calcareous tufa stone, the temples glow with a golden warmth at sunset. They were actually set on fire by the Carthaginians in 406 BC and restored by the Romans in the first century AD, respecting the original Doric style. The final collapse of the temples was the result either of earthquakes or of the destructive fury of the Christians, acting on an edict of the Eastern Emperor Theodosius in the fourth century. The only one still relatively intact is the Temple of Concord, which was transformed into a church in the sixth century. It is one of the best-preserved temples from ancient times, both elegant and impressive, and a fine example of what is called 'optical correction': the columns are tapered, growing slimmer towards the top so as to seem taller, and they have an entasis, a slight swelling, about two-thirds of the way up, which counteracts the optical effect of the tapering. They are also slightly inclined towards the centre of the façade, so as to present a perfectly straight image to the eye. During the Middle Ages the temples were plundered for building material, and the Temple of Zeus was actually referred to as the Giants' Quarry. Near the Temple of Heracles stands the Villa Aurea, once the residence of Sir Alexander Hardcastle, a passionate British patron of archaeology who financed the raising of the columns.

Along this long south-western coast at night the lights on the fishing-boats twinkle out at sea as they no doubt did when the temples were built over 2000 years ago. A few years ago I had a chance to see the Greek temples of Selinunte from a novel viewpoint: swimming slowly in the sea in front of them, without a care in my mind … They stood, motionless; even if houses and blocks of flats had multiplied all around them, it was as if they alone existed, immobile in some timeless dimension. Now when I holiday here, I spend hours on the empty beach with my children where we play endless games of building 'Venice' in the sand, with canals that quickly fill with more sand and palaces that are swallowed by the waves.

Also in conflict with time are the remains of the villages and towns of the valley of Belice, razed by an earthquake in 1968. One of these was Gibellina, rebuilt (nearer the motorway) about 20 kilometres from the ruins of the old town; the ruins themselves were transformed into a disturbing piece of landscape art by Alberto Burri, a sculptor from Umbria. He covered the rubble with a great wave of cement, broken by deep crevasses that follow the lines of the ancient roads, like a maze of stone; in this tomb of the city the voices of its old inhabitants still seem to hang in the air, modulated by wild flowers growing in the cracks.

Not far away lay two Greek cities with a long history of conflict. In 413 BC the umpteenth attempt by Selinunte to penetrate the territory of Segesta triggered a war that involved the great

PAGES 182 AND 183: The grandiose Greek temple at Segesta, not far from Palermo, is immensely impressive, standing alone in the barren landscape. The 36 columns of the peristyle are over 9 metres high and are almost 2 metres wide at the base.
OPPOSITE: The amphitheatre at Segesta looks like a precious sea shell on top of a hill, with the sea in the distance beyond it.
BELOW: *Il Cretto* by Alberto Burri – cement moulded like a tomb covering the earthquake ruins of Gibellina, south of Segesta.

powers of the time. Segesta sought help from Athens and Carthage, while Selinunte turned to Syracuse, Agrigento and Gela. The Carthaginian general Hannibal tried to resolve the dispute between the two cities by diplomatic means, but Selinunte rejected the attempts at arbitration. So in 409 BC Hannibal and a massive force of infantry and cavalry broke into the city, sacking and pillaging it, and slaughtering the population. Women and children took refuge in the temples, while a few other inhabitants managed to flee to Agrigento. For Selinunte, all that was left was oblivion. Today, the only traces of one of the most famous Greek colonies of western Sicily are the remnants of a few temples, together with the nearby quarry at Cusa where the various stages of the extraction and processing of tufa can still be seen among the olive groves and almond orchards.

TUNA, SALT AND WINE

Westwards from here lies Mazara del Vallo, a colony of Selinunte, which was destroyed by the Carthaginians, taken over by the Romans and then flourished under the Arabs. In 1998, just offshore at a depth of 500 metres, some fishermen found a life-size bronze statue of a dancing satyr, represented in mid-leap: a mythological figure from the orgiastic procession that accompanied Dionysius. Mazara is now one of the great Mediterranean centres of the swordfish and tuna industry. The so-called 'racing tuna' come into the waters here when they are still brawny and muscular; they then grow fat and give birth and at this point man comes in and slaughters them. When I buy fish here I want to haggle, as one would do for a carpet; we're not that far from North Africa, after all.

During World War II my grandfather, Duca Francesco Vanni d'Archirafi, who had fought bravely at the battles of the Carso and the Piave in World War I at the age of 20, was in command of the coastline between Marsala and Mazara del Vallo, and inland to Castelvetrano. My mother, who was a child at the time, has told me countless stories about this period. Crown Prince Umberto once came to visit and she overheard my father point out that the various look-out bunkers, built as defence against an invasion, could do very little to hold off an attack. An elegant dinner service, which ever afterwards was known jokingly as 'Umberto's service', had been taken from the house to the command-post to be used for the royal lunch. She also recalls the day when my grandfather came home and asked my grandmother how much money they had, since no funds had been sent to pay the soldiers and he was going to advance them a little money himself because they had 'families to support'.

Marsala, where Garibaldi and his thousand followers landed in 1860 — the action that best sums up the unification of Italy — lies a little west of Mazara. The name is Arabic for the Port of Allah. In 1773 a ship carrying a merchant from Liverpool, John Woodhouse, was forced to take shelter in its harbour because of bad weather. Woodhouse had come to Sicily to buy soda ash, but in a tavern he tasted and liked the local wine, made from grapes grown in the area around

OPPOSITE: Ernesto Basile, master of the Liberty style in Palermo during the early twentieth century, often collaborated with Ducrot for boiserie and Ettore De Maria Bergler for murals. This is an example from Villa Igiea, which is now a top hotel, but was used as an emergency hospital by English soldiers during World War II.

THE ENGLISH
IN SICILY

DURING THE EIGHTEENTH AND NINETEENTH CENTURIES a number of English families moved to Sicily for business purposes. One of these was the Whitaker family; their business was founded by one Benjamin Ingham, who had come to Palermo from Yorkshire at the age of 22. He first worked in the wine trade in Marsala, but soon extended his concerns to oil, citrus fruits, velvet and silk. He invited his sister's sons to join him, one of whom, Joseph Whitaker, proved to be a perfect manager. In 1837 Joseph married Sophia Sanderson, the daughter of a businessman in Messina. Obliged to live in the stifling city of Palermo with their 12 children, some years later the couple bought a property from the Marchesi di Mazzarino, a villa near the Favorita park, which they named the Villa Sofia.

On Whitaker's death the business passed into the hands of his three sons, who had decided to remain in Sicily. Joseph, known as Pip, lived in the Villa Malfitano, where he and his wife Tina Scalia dedicated themselves to charity and philanthropy. In 1897 they set up a charity called the Humanitarian and Educational Society for Abandoned Children and for the Protection of Animals. The dual purpose of the society offended a number of Palermitans, who were indignant at children being put on the same level as animals, and Whitaker felt obliged to change its name.

Another son, Joshua, known as Joss, settled in the Villa Whitaker (now the Prefecture), while the third son, Robert, took up residence in the Villa Sofia. He restructured the building in the fashionable Art Nouveau taste of the time – known in Italy as *Stile Liberty*, after the shop in London that was at the forefront of this design movement. It changed the face of Palermo within two decades. One fine example is Villa Igiea (now a hotel), named after the goddess of health (Hygeia), at the foot of Mount Pellegrino, which the leading entrepreneurial family, the Florios, transformed from a neo-Gothic building to a luxurious residence in Art Nouveau style. At Robert's behest a tower and further extensions were added to the Villa Sofia, including a Cavallerizza, a pool-filled stonework and iron pavilion with a majolica floor, which served as a winter garden – he was a keen botanist who collected orchids and other exotic plants. But when Robert died, the Villa Sofia fell into decline in the hands of his two daughters. After the failure of her first marriage, his daughter Boots married an American and left Palermo; the other, Aileen, sold the villa due to financial pressures.

When Italy entered World War II on the German side in 1940, the Whitakers, still British citizens, had the majority of their property confiscated. Only the Villa Malfitano stayed in their hands, because it had been registered in the name of Pip's wife, who was Sicilian.

Marsala and in the province of Trapani. He bought several barrels, and to make the wine survive a voyage home of several weeks he fortified it by adding alcohol. This was the origin of Marsala; the trade started with Woodhouse and continued first with Benjamin Ingham, then the Whitakers and finally the Florio family, who made the sweet dessert wine of that name famous throughout the world. The wine is still made using techniques invented by the Phoenicians.

Not far from Marsala is a lagoon known as the Stagnone, or Big Pond, containing shallow water rich in salt. Along the road here are a number of salt-works: sheets of water subdivided by thin strips of earth form an irregular and multi-coloured chessboard, with windmills to grind the salt and pump the water. These workings have been here for some 2000 years since the days of the Phoenicians, who exported salt throughout the Mediterranean and fished for sea anemones and murex shellfish with which they made a purple textile dye. The systematic exploitation of this piece of land became so profitable that in 1800 it was made a monopoly of the Crown.

On an island in the Stagnone is Mozia, formerly Motya, the Phoenician fortress-city that remained uninhabited after it was destroyed in 397 BC by order of the tyrant of Syracuse, Dionysius. The short stretch of lagoon that separates it from the mainland was once regularly crossed by grape-laden carts drawn by oxen, which had to wade through water a metre deep. Some of the great slabs of stone that paved the old road still reappear at low tide.

Thucydides, a Greek author of the fifth century BC, recounts that the Phoenicians, traders in the Aegean since the second millennium BC, had made their way into the western Mediterranean and occupied coastal promontories and the nearby islets for the purpose of trading. Later, around the eighth to the seventh century BC, following the arrival of the Greeks the Phoenicians, 'after abandoning most of their stations, drew together and went to live in Motya, Soloeis, and Panormus, near the Elymi', who were their allies. These places were all conveniently situated for the voyage to Carthage in modern Tunisia, the Mediterranean homeland of the Phoenicians.

In 397 BC Dionysius, who intended to consolidate his rule in Sicily, made war against the colonies of Carthage. Assistance from home took too long to reach Motya. Having built a kind of temporary quay, Dionysius brought his war machines right up to the walls of the city. The Motyans fought fiercely: they feared the enemy's revenge, because in the past the Phoenicians had treated Greek prisoners very cruelly. But in the end Dionysius' army prevailed. 'A great deal of silver, some gold, luxurious garments and a great quantity of other valuable objects were obtained, while Dionysius sold off the Motyan survivors as booty,' wrote Diodorus Siculus, in the first century AD.

OLD SICILIAN SOCIETY

The remains of Motya were rediscovered at the end of the nineteenth century by Joseph Whitaker; and the extensive ruins of the Phoenician settlement together with the marvellous statue of a 'young ephebe', a proudly poised figure in a pleated tunic, can be seen in a museum in one of the former Whitaker family homes. It is said that when they held parties at another of their houses, the Villa Amalfitana, and guests stayed too late, Whitaker would drop the none-too-subtle hint: 'If I were at your home now, I'd go to my home.' This seems like English manners superimposed on Sicilian hospitality. At Palazzo Butera, the Princess of Trabia had her own way of making it clear to guests that it was time they took their leave: at midnight the butler would bring her a cup of camomile tea. Sicilians can be clear and direct, though not rude – as, for instance, the gentleman who said to a man who was paying rather too much attention to his wife: 'I see that you like my wife, but then so do I.'

Another Sicilian trait is a sense of fun. My great-aunt Lilly Rosalia was apparently the first woman in Palermo to own and drive a car; it was quite small, and during a party some

THE FLORIO DYNASTY

IN THE NINETEENTH CENTURY Sicily's biggest name in business was that of Florio. They began as 'outsiders' from the Calabrian mainland, where Paolo Florio was a shrewd trader in spices, medicinal drugs and colonial goods with a keen eye on the markets throughout Europe. After a major earthquake Calabria hit hard times; Palermo, on the other hand, was still the seat of a king (albeit with reduced powers) and the city was growing culturally and financially, even though the island was still a hungry land, with a perpetual conflict between the aristocratic landowners and the great army of the poor. There was no middle class to speak of, but the Florios moved in and soon established themselves.

When Paolo's son Vincenzo, who had travelled throughout Europe to learn several languages and study the family's most profitable lines of business, took over the firm his first business hunch was to focus on the sale of cinchona. The Florios sold this remedy for malaria in their grocery shops, much to the indignation of pharmacists. It was the first demonstration of the family's capacity to make courageous entrepreneurial decisions, while the native Sicilian tendency was just to let things happen according to destiny.

In 1833 Vincenzo, by now an expert in foreign trade, bought a piece of land in Marsala between the vineyards of Ingham and Woodhouse, openly competing with the English merchants. He built his own vineyard, but it was 20 years before he began to make a profit. No matter – the family's business interests were by then widely diversified and firmly established in the area of shipping activities since Florio was principal shareholder of the Navigazione Generale Italiana, which with 106 steamships

was almost as big as the entire Italian merchant fleet. All those in authority, from the Bourbons downwards, stipulated contracts with the Florios for the transport of travellers, of emigrants (to North and South America), of goods or of troops – for example to Africa, when the Italian army was sent off to gain an empire but ended up being slaughtered at the battle of Adowa in Ethiopia in 1896.

Now wealthier than ever before, and fascinated by the aristocracy, Vincenzo was very successful in marrying all his children into the most important Sicilian families. The Florios had their own private train as well as several fashionable villas built for them in Palermo by the eminent Art Nouveau architect Ernesto Basile. Vincenzo's son, Ignazio Junior, married Franca Jacona Notarbartolo who was considered one of the most beautiful women of the Italian elite. Ignazio Junior, however, was destined to prove the truth of the old saying about the rich: the first generation starts things off, the second one keeps them going and the third one destroys them.

A friend of writers and painters, Ignazio read Nietzsche, d'Annunzio and Marinetti, but his real passion was women. His affairs became legendary: yachts and jewels slipped through his

fingers, given away to dancers after ten minutes' acquaintance. Although there was more to Ignazio than just the *bon viveur*, fate was against him: in 1920 the firm that made Marsala was taken over by Cinzano. The Ignazio Florio china factory, opened in the late 1880s, went into crisis and in the 1940s was taken over by Richard Ginori. Politics went badly for him too: two ministers – Sicilians supporting northern industries – cancelled provisions for shipowners and the Florios' shipping interests were ceded to the Tirrenia shipping line, which was later taken over by the Institute for Industrial Reconstruction during the Fascist period.

In an attempt to resist destiny, with malicious stories also circulating about his private life, Vincenzo had founded a new daily newspaper, *L'Ora*, in 1900 in an attempt to influence public opinion. To no avail. Ignazio, known as the 'dissipator', lived much longer than any of his predecessors but without leaving any male descendants. He is said to have spent his final years watching the Tirrenia ships disappear over the horizon.

ABOVE: Contestants in the first Targa Florio race 100 years ago. It is still an annual event.

of her friends actually carried it away and hid it. It isn't only Italian *men* who are infatuated with fast cars! This redoubtable lady took part in the Targa Florio car race, a thrilling event that takes place along mountain roads to the north of Palermo. This, the oldest car race in the world, was inaugurated in 1906 by the Florio family and was described by the great racing driver Juan Manuel Fangio as 'not just a race but a party'. No wonder my great-aunt enjoyed herself! But my grandmother, Nonna Delia, must have been less enthralled. Frightened by the speed, she spent the whole race beating the driver over the head with the spare tyre.

Sicilians have a taste for paradox. I heard a story that a friend of my Palermo relatives, being without his butler for a while, sent himself a telegram every day so that the postman would wake him up instead. Another one would bury himself in his library for the afternoon, studying atlases and historical documents, and then say that he had been on a fascinating trip to these places. Every noble family reputedly kept a room in the mental hospital run by the Capuchin friars, because one never knew when it might be needed – just like the bust of Abbot Meli, an eminent Sicilian historian, which was always used in the old gentlemen's club of Palermo as a spare dinner guest whenever there was the risk of 13 at the table.

My grandfather was also a source of some fairly caustic stories, for instance: 'There was a man who was having an affair with a married woman and they always met in his bachelor pad. And so a group of friends, during one of their amorous encounters, called in a bricklayer and got him to wall up the door, imprisoning the couple inside!' But then he concluded: 'One

ABOVE: The opulent interor of the Palazzo Aiutamicristo in Palermo, now owned by the Baroni Calefati di Canalotti. Guglielmo Aiutamicristo, a Pisan banker, built the palace in the 1400s when he moved to the capital from the family's Arabian castle in the countryside, in order to better manage his thriving export business, specializing in cheeses and Sicilian grains.

named the sin but never the sinners – it was another age.' My grandfather recalled nostalgically, 'It was when the Botanical Gardens of Palermo were still part our own grounds, and then "flights of swallows ... ".' This Sicilian term refers to the dissipation of family wealth. The botanical gardens are now owned by the university.

This was just the frivolous surface of Sicilian society – a society made up of people who would devote themselves to the serious study of astronomy, botany, literature, history, heraldry, agriculture and so on, and who were ready to die for their country if needed. They were brought up with a great sense of duty, not just a belief in their right to pleasure. But those words murmured by my grandfather resounded silently like those of Don Fabrizio in *The Leopard*. The author of this novel, the aristocrat Giuseppe Tomasi di Lampedusa, recounted the end of a world and the extinction of a caste; a great opportunity missed with the nineteenth-century annexation of Sicily to Italy. His is the story of the old Sicilian aristocracy, the nostalgic expression of the egoism of a dying class that mistook its own decline for the decline of all values, of life itself. They passed on the reins of power to new people who were only interested in a quick profit, but who managed to pass themselves off as a new patriotic ruling class. *The Leopard* depicts this new order in all its falsity and triviality.

PALERMO: SCENES FROM FAMILY LIFE

I don't remember my first visit to Palermo, and so it's as if I've always been going there. My mother was born in this city and lived there until she got married at the age of 23, and so every year, usually at Christmas, we would travel down to see grandparents, uncles and aunts, cousins and other relatives. We would drive onto the mail-boat at Naples and arrive, with luck, on the island the next morning. I say 'with luck' because at the port of Naples they often loaded the cars and lorries so haphazardly that some would get left on shore. And then they would have to do it all over again, late into the night. But we always managed to get there even if we never knew exactly when.

People who wanted to be absolutely sure of getting a place would sit on the bonnets of other cars about to drive onto the ferry, in an attempt to stop them. On one occasion, the owner of a luxurious car climbed onto our bonnet and my mother, with my brother and myself inside, zoomed off with the intruder still *in situ*. It took him completely by surprise and he started a terrible row, accusing my mother of trying to kill him.

I had never considered her to be so daring, not even when I enquired into her past: in keeping with Sicilian traditions, she had not been able to go to university because there was no one to accompany her and she couldn't go by herself. It was only by pure chance that she met my father, at a lunch party out in the country; she was rarely able to accept such invitations in a place where even today long tablecloths are hung over the railings of balconies to prevent those

OPPOSITE: The planting of the Botanical Gardens in Palermo has been assiduously arranged according to distinct classification systems. There is also a section devoted to 'useful plants', which includes these trees from the same family as the African baobab. The Botanical Gardens were created on ground previously owned by the Sicilian branch of my family. OVERLEAF: A panorama of Palermo at daybreak.

ABOVE: The faded glory of Palermo is evident wherever you look. It may seem quaint to visitors, but living here is another thing entirely. OPPOSITE: Behind Monreale Cathedral its ornate Norman apse looms large, creating a special, magical atmosphere.

below seeing the legs of unmarried women. Sicilian women, and women from outside who marry Sicilians and settle on the island, are appreciated if they learn to keep their eyes lowered.

The boat was often late and in the morning the extra hours out at sea would give me the chance to get to know some of the other passengers. If I got talking to a girl of my own age who, like me, was on her way to see relatives, shyness would always prevent me from asking for her telephone number; I would then spend the whole holiday hoping to bump into her again. So journeys were also a sentimental dream; often these girls had blue eyes and blonde hair that suggested distant Norman ancestry.

I don't know why, but the pleasant sense of having arrived in Palermo (or 'Palemmo', as my uncle pronounced it) always began for me as we turned up the long Corso Vittorio Emanuele, the start of the 8-kilometre-long road, the city's main thoroughfare, that runs, under various names, all the way from the sea up to the cathedral of Monreale, one of the pearls of Norman art. To describe some of the sights that lie along this street as it carves its way inland is as good an introduction to Palermo as any.

THE NORMAN
ARCHITECTURAL
LEGACY

THE NAME MONREALE derives from the Latin *mons regalis*, meaning 'mountain worthy of the king'. Originally it was just an Arab hamlet near a spring. Then it became the Arab seat of government, where Roger II subsequently built the Norman equivalent, the royal palace. The place achieved its fame, however, after 1174, when Roger's son William had the abbey and monastery built. According to legend William, hunting in the countryside outside Palermo, stopped to rest in the shade of a carob tree. The Virgin Mary then appeared to him in a dream, pointing to the site of hidden treasure that he was to use to build a church.

William hired Arab masons and Byzantine and Burgundian artists and mosaicists to work on the great cathedral and its splendid cloisters, a fascinating mixture of Islamic, Byzantine and Romanesque architecture. The façade has two lofty square towers and a portal with columns in the Doric style, above which are arches in calcarean and lava stone. The dazzling gold mosaics along the walls of the aisles were executed in the twelfth and thirteenth centuries and represent the cycle of the Old and New Testaments, with inscriptions in Latin and Greek.

In the central apse appears the magnificent image of the Benedictory Christ with the Greek word 'Pantocrator' (Omnipotent) beneath it, emblem of the majesty of this sacred building.

In the Norman palace the figurative dynamism of the mosaics contributes to their symbolic meanings, with vivid Byzantine peacocks portrayed alongside the birds of the Koran. An example of the union of different Christian rites can be seen in the figures of the two Christs in the Palatine Chapel: the one in the dome is blessing with his fingers held downwards, in accordance with Greek symbolism; the fingers of the Christ Pantocrator in the apse point up, in accordance with Latin ritual. This symbolism had a very specific meaning: Roger II was the divine interpreter and the consecrated priest, crowned in the mosaics by Christ himself, around whom everything revolved. The figure of the king is made from precious marbles, and above the throne area appears the figure of Christ.

Roger II de Hauteville possessed exceptional political skills and a lively imagination. At the beginning of his reign, Palermo and indeed the whole of Sicily were characterized by ethnic and religious differences. His political astuteness led him to tolerate these differences, so that Muslim Arabs, Orthodox Greeks, Catholics and Jews co-existed peacefully, just as the architecture of his buildings combined the Byzantine, Arab, Roman and Norman military styles.

In both its architectural forms and its mosaic decoration the Palatine Chapel displays all these different tendencies. The plan of the building is based on a synthesis between the squarer form of the Byzantine basilica and the Latin style based on a long nave. The Arab component can be seen in the wooden ceiling, the most ancient example of *muqarnas* (which symbolizes forgiveness) formed by a myriad of honeycomb locules carved in 1131 by Eastern craftsmen,

ABOVE: A mosaic detail from Monreale Cathedral depicting a scene from the life of St Castrensis.
OPPOSITE: The magnificent central apse of Monreale Cathedral, with Christ Pantocrator.

ABOVE AND RIGHT: The splendid cloister of the Benedictine abbey alone would make Monreale extraodinary, with its 228 columns, some meticulously carved, many with mosaic inlay.
OPPOSITE TOP: The church of San Giovanni degli Eremiti, fusing Norman and Arabian architecture.
OPPOSITE BELOW: The Zisa, a pleasure palace.

decorated with paintings in which the human figure is mingled with the symbolic shapes of animals and abstract patterns.

One of the most characteristic monuments of Norman Palermo, also erected by Roger II in 1132, is San Giovanni degli Eremiti, set in a tiny garden with a magical atmosphere. The church is a plain square building with a single-arched bell-tower and five small red domes which look decidedly oriental. The fascination of the interior derives from the play of light and shadow created by the interaction between the domes and the side walls, the pointed arches and the corner niches. There is also a small thirteenth-century cloister, which has twin columns along one side.

The Zisa (from Arabic El Aziz, meaning 'noble' or 'splendid') is another impressive Norman building on the appropriately named Via dei Normanni. Begun by William I 'the Bad', son of the great Roger II, this castle was completed by William II. It contains a funeral plaque made by a priest for his mother, and written in four languages – Arabic, Greek, Latin and Hebrew – which demonstrates yet again the cosmopolitan nature of society in the Norman period. When William I built the Zisa he wanted it to be both a place of pleasure and an expression of the king's power. The extraordinary compositional unity of the exterior achieves the latter aim by the rigour of its architectural lines, while the interior caters for the royal leisure with an extensive harem and fountains gushing into octagonal basins and flowing towards the once magnificent garden. These water-filled gardens formed the 'Earthly Paradise', known as the Genoard, planted with orange and lemon trees and cedars. The combination of gardens and water, characteristic of many Norman buildings, suggests the balance between nature, the divine and the works of man.

In 1565, during the Spanish rule of Sicily, the port was enlarged westwards by Viceroy Garcia Alvarez de Toledo, son of Fernando, Duke of Alba, and an ancestor of my paternal grandmother, Eugenia de Vito Piscicelli of Collesano. After leaving the port area the street immediately runs into elegant Piazza Marina, with the Giardino Garibaldi at its centre. These gardens were laid out in the mid-nineteenth century by the architect Giovanni Battista Basile.

This is the place where a man named Joe Petrosino was killed, among the *Ficus magnolides* trees. He was a police lieutenant from New York, though of Sicilian origin, who had come back home to help fight the Mafia. In 1873 he emigrated to America as a child with his family. Joe learned to speak English, tried his hand at numerous trades, and in 1883 enrolled in the New York police force. He single-mindedly applied all his passion, instinct and intelligence to his great aim of defeating the Mafia and its American offshoot, the Black Hand. By clever undercover work he managed to penetrate their complex and secretive world, delivering important bosses into the hands of the law and thus earning the appreciation of President Theodore Roosevelt, who promoted him personally to sergeant in 1895. Having travelled to Europe to examine the relationships between the American and Sicilian organizations, Petrosino set in motion a major operation that was intended to finish the Mafia off for good. But in March 1909 they caught up with him in Palermo in the Giardino Garibaldi and shot him dead.

It was on the orders of the same Viceroy Garcia Alvarez who extended the port that the road leading from it, once the road of the ancient Càssaro, was extended. The name derived from the Arabic El Kasr – castle – referring to the ancient fortress built by the Emir at the time when Palermo was known as the city of the 500 mosques, together with the citadel of Kalsa or Al Halish. Under the Spanish this great artery was driven through the centre of the city, gutting the maze of streets and alleys in the old medieval quarter; the centre was redeveloped following a much simplified pattern that reflected the Spanish desire for control and dominion. Grandiose palaces were built, too, transforming the appearance of the city. Now, however, after the bombardments of World War II, often little more than façades remain; in more than half a century they have been neither restored nor demolished.

It was under the Emperor Charles V, who made his triumphal entrance into Palermo in 1535, that the Spaniards embarked on major works of urban renovation, reinforcing the fortified walls and building the castle ramparts. For nearly 200 years, having already experienced Arab,

ABOVE: With my mischievous son Pierangelo, playing hide-and-seek among the monumental *Ficus* trees in Piazza Marina.
OPPOSITE: Mythological figures adorn the enormous circular fountain in Piazza Pretoria, which nearly fills the square.

Norman, German and French rule, and despite the insurrection of Palermo and Messina in the mid-seventeenth century, Sicily remained a Spanish viceroyalty. And then in 1714, at the end of the War of Spanish Succession, it was assigned to the Savoy dynasty. But in 1720 they exchanged it for Sardinia, so that Sicily was reunited with southern Italy under the dominion of Austria. With the Peace of Vienna in 1738 the Bourbons succeeded the Austrians and remained in power until 1860, when Sicily became part of the new kingdom of Italy. It is scarcely surprising that, with such a history, the island should display such a multiplicity of cultural influences in its art, buildings, customs, food, speech and many other aspects of Sicilian life.

Proceeding inland along the great thoroughfare, we find the fountain of Piazza Pretoria, created in 1554 by the Florentine sculptor Francesco Camilliani. The piazza is also known as the 'Place of Shame' due to the numerous nude statues it contains – but also alluding, with typical Sicilian irony, to the misdeeds and misappropriations perpetrated over the centuries by the city's rulers, who governed Palermo from headquarters situated here. The fountain is elliptical in form, with three levels of concentric basins decorated with mythological statues symbolizing the four rivers of the city. It was originally intended for the Florentine villa of Don Pietro di Toledo, a relative of the viceroy mentioned above, but in 1573 his son Luigi, maybe because of transport problems, sold it to the Palermo Senate for 30,000 *scudi* – which would have sufficed to build an entire villa. It had to fulfil a double function: as a 'sacred object' for Palermo and as a central point in the 'urban cosmology'.

This crossroads, where the long road to Monreale meets the long road parallel to the coast, became Piazza Vigliena, named after the Viceroy Don Francisco Fernandez Pacheco, Marquis of Vigliena. The square is grandiose and theatrical, celebratory and symbolic in its layout. Known as the Quattro Canti (Four Corners), with its seventeenth-century Baroque architecture it is the very hub of Palermo, a kind of spatial synthesis of the whole city. Its architecture is typical of the kind that was developing throughout Europe at that time. In the corners four tiered statues each represent one of the seasons, a Spanish viceroy, and, on the upper level, one of the four Palermitan saints, each one acting as protectress of the quarter of the city that lies behind her.

Further along the street the cathedral comes into view. A Norman-Sicilian jewel, it was built in 1185 on the site of a previous basilica, transformed by the Arabs into a mosque, then restored to the Christian faith by the Normans. It was built at the same time as the cathedral of Monreale and there was said to be great competition between them, with spies being sent up and down the mountain to observe the development of the rival building. But the cathedral was remodelled between the fourteenth and sixteenth centuries and even more drastically in the nineteenth, when the Florentine Ferdinando Fuga disfigured it with an ill-suited dome in place of the tower. Giuseppe Pitrè, in *La Vita di Palermo cento e più anni fa* (*Life in Palermo a hundred and more years ago*), wrote bleakly: 'As we go towards Porta Nuova we hide our eyes so as not to see the Cathedral.'

Fuga also transformed the interior of the cathedral, where in a majestic porphyry mausoleum Frederick II of Swabia is supposed to be buried. However Thomas of Eccleston, an English chronicler who lived at the time of the Sicilian-German emperor, tells of a spectacular ceremony as the sovereign's body was accompanied into the crater of Etna, from which he was to rise as Anti-Christ to fight his last battle at the end of time. The sober voice of history instead recounts that Frederick was actually laid to rest in the cathedral of Palermo, the burial-place of other Norman and Aragon rulers, on 25 February 1251, two months after his death from dysentery in Puglia on the southern Italian mainland. Subsequently, during the 1260s, Sicily passed into the hands of the Angevin French who imposed a harsh and disciplinarian regime. The island eventually threw off this yoke after the revolt of 1282 known as the Sicilian Vespers, during which a massacre of Angevins took place. The rebels asked Peter III of Aragon for help, and after the Angevins were finally expelled the island was assigned to his son Frederick, who took the title of King of Trinacria. Sicily thus came under the rule of Spain for the first time.

The street, now called Corso Calatafimi, passes close to the 'catacombs' in the cemetery of the Capuchins, near the Porta Nuova. I still remember visiting it as a child, and seeing the skeletons of friars and nuns, and of men, women and children of rank, hanging on hooks by their feet or by the neck, in garments that reflect their social status. A popular legend recounts that, when a calamity strikes Palermo, the friars come down from their hooks and wander through the city.

To reach the cathedral of Monreale, its ultimate destination, the Corso follows a series of hairpin bends embellished with stone exedras and fountains: truly curious on an island where

water is so scarce! Teobaldo, the first abbot of Monreale, which was bestowed on him by the Norman King William II, headed an archdiocese of great political importance, governed as it was by members of leading families such as the Medici and the Farnese, the Borgia and the Colonna, the Orsini and the nobility of Spain and France. The archdiocese gradually grew, taking in the three castles of Giato, Corleone (now better known for its Mafia clan) and Calatosi, with concessions on vineyards, market gardens, mills and tuna fisheries.

CHILDHOOD MEMORIES

This long, straight road between the sea and the mountain is not so very different from those in other Sicilian cities, towns and villages. Behind the shutters everyone is watching, a thousand eyes are secretly on the look-out. But should anyone ever be questioned, they either weren't there or they were asleep at the time.

This is a feeling that a certain Filippo Bentivegna from Sciacca on the west coast managed – perhaps unwittingly – to capture in stone. There were thousands of stones on his *podere* (smallholding), and the faces that he carved onto them gaze into the distance, into the void – or maybe into your own self. Bentivegna was a simple labourer who emigrated to America to make some money. He stayed there for a while, then got into a quarrel over a woman and was hit on the head, which affected him mentally. He decided to return to his native Sciacca where he bought his smallholding and started to carve. When the stones ran out, Bentivegna started to dig caves and tunnels in the ground in search of more. Considered just another harmless lunatic, he was left in

THE ORIGINS OF THE MAFIA

THE TERM *MAFIOSO* was first used in the title of a dramatic comedy, *The Mafiosi of Vicaria*, in 1860. *Mafiosi* were portrayed as the most respectable inmates of prisons, and by 1875 nearly all European languages recognized the term.

The formation of the Mafia reflects the social changes to Sicilian feudalism during the reunification of Italy in the nineteenth century. Landowners, usually noblemen, had land agents who managed the rent of their lands to peasant farmers. Rents became such that the agents gained power at the expense of the landowners, and they appropriated certain rights by colluding with the police and courts, even creating their own security forces. They were left 'untouched' by the new Italian state – physically and psychologically so far away that it hadn't closed the gaps left by the demise of feudalism.

The Mafia had become the only effective authority in Sicily, protecting noblemen and peasants alike from third-party intimidation – in exchange for *pizzu* (money) and their under-taking to cast the 'right vote'. As a consequence, elected parliamentarians obstructed the passage of 'anti-Mafia' laws.

During World War I the 'men of honour' enriched themselves while providing the Italian army with supplies. This reinforced their powers, and they were regarded as the 'new nobility'. Under Fascism, the Mafia financed Mussolini who, once he was elected, turned tail and sent a prefect to Sicily to wipe out the Mafia. He failed because the Mafia were already too well connected.

During World War II contact between American and Sicilian branches supported the Allied landings in Sicily in July 1943. It is said that the subsequent advance northwards up the peninsula was smoother for the Americans than the British due to links between the American secret services and the Mafia.

ABOVE: Mafiosi figurines in a tourist shop.
BELOW: A street in the Vucciria market. Its name, in dialect, translates as 'voices' or 'hubbub'.

peace. He continued to sculpt for the rest of his life, expecting to be addressed as 'Your Excellency' because in his mind the little farm had become a castle and the sculptures were his subjects.

In the years when we visited Sicily things were far from peaceful; the 1980s were characterized by what was referred to as the *mattanza*, a term originally used to describe the slaughter of tuna, which were caught in a sort of water-chamber and then killed with harpoons. A Mafia war was then raging among the various bands or *cosche*. *Cosca*, the Sicilian word for a Mafia family, literally means an artichoke and symbolizes the way the members of a family are bound tightly together around a single centre. At that time the clan of the Corleonesi exterminated the rival clans, killing over a thousand people. Some idea of their determination and cruelty can be gleaned from the story of Tommaso Buscetta. He was a boss of one of the losing *cosche* and became a *pentito*, or turncoat, collaborating with the law; at this point the Mafia decided to eliminate all his relatives to the twentieth degree of consanguinity, excluding only children under the age of four. Many of them were tied hand and foot and thrown into car boots in such a way that if they moved they would kill themselves. But, as the *pentiti* put it, it was all just a 'squabble among neighbours'.

My mother's family villa is on Corso Calatafimi, at Mezzo Monreale (halfway to Monreale), just a stone's throw from the Cubala, a small, cube-shaped building with a red dome and ogival arches open on all four sides; it was one of the pavilions of the old park of William II. Year after year new buildings have sprung up along the road, transforming this part of the plain from open countryside into a buzzing suburb. The house, an eighteenth-century villa, was badly damaged by fire in the mid-nineteenth century. Nearby lived a famous woman patriot known as La Farina; in 1848, the year of revolutions that shook the whole of Europe, she took an active part in the anti-Bourbon events in Sicily. When the uprising was repressed, it was decreed that her house should be burnt down in punishment – but unfortunately the authorities got the wrong house. Ironically our villa, the one that did get burnt, belonged to Bourbon supporters.

Like the kingdom of Naples, during the Napoleonic period Sicily was under the rule of the French Marshal Murat, but his regime ended in 1815 with the fall of Napoleon. When the two states were unified under the name of the Kingdom of the Two Sicilies this loss of autonomy led to the anti-Bourbon insurrection of 1820. It was swiftly crushed, but the struggle returned some 40 years later. The revolt against the hated Bourbons broke out on the morning of 4 April 1860, signalled by the bell of the convent of Gancia. It was suppressed rapidly and with great brutality. Many people were killed and others were imprisoned along with the monks; only two conspirators escaped the slaughter, hiding for five days in the burial ground of the convent. Finally, in desperation, they piled up a few coffins, climbed on top and showed their faces at a window-grating. They were spotted and people came to their aid, blocking the road with carts to prevent the Bourbon troops from seeing what was going on. The two men were then pulled out through a narrow hole, since known as the Hole of Salvation, in Via Alloro.

BELOW: The Cubala is set in the Norman Royal Park. These gardens, including the original irrigation system and citrus plantation, have recently been restored.

ABOVE: My Sicilian grandfather with my brother, my cousins and me (front left), when I was about five years old.

That year, 1860, was also the year of Garibaldi's Expedition of the Thousand. This seaborne invasion, aided by the *picciotti*, the Sicilian rebels, defeated the Bourbons and drove them out. Meanwhile, the Royal Navy, anchored just offshore, was under orders not to intervene despite the fact that Britain was an ally of the Kingdom of the Two Sicilies. After the proclamation of the kingdom of Italy in 1866 there was another insurrection, this time aimed at Sicilian secession, but it too was quickly put down.

I remember from my childhood a Sicilian great-great-great uncle telling a story that fascinated me. An ancestor of his wanted to go on a pilgrimage to the Holy Land to fulfil a vow of gratitude that he had taken on escaping a cholera epidemic. He did not have enough money for the enterprise, so he decided to make the journey within his own house and grounds. And so one Monday evening he set off with his butler and retinue for the Holy Land. One night they camped near the goldfish pond with the papyrus plants grazing the tent-cloth, the next by the flowerbed under the blossoming orange trees. Gradually they made their way from the stables to the ballroom, the music room and so on, making as many circuits as were necessary to complete the distance, until they finally 'reached' the Holy Land. To celebrate the event a thanksgiving Mass was held in the chapel of the house. As soon as it was over my ancestor turned to his butler: 'Time to make our way home again.'

Very deferentially the butler replied, 'Sir, if you don't mind I would prefer to stay here in the Holy Land.'

This story inspired a play with a different ending. The prince, having walked seven 'cursed paces' less than the real distance, died and was doomed to spend eternity looking for the mistake in his calculations. 'Those above know where and how I went wrong, but of course they won't tell me: I have to find it out by myself, and only when I discover the right point, identifying it down to the millimetre, will the gates of Paradise open up for me.'

He was, it seems, not the only eccentric in the family. It is said that another relative left his town house to go to the villa in Corso Calatafimi, which was then in the country, in order to wind all the clocks and feed the pigeons with a bagful of food. At least that was his story – because it seems that his bag actually contained a hoard of gold coins, which he buried somewhere along the way. I think my cousins who now live there are still searching for them!

On our arrival at the family villa, having driven along the great thoroughfare from the port, we would ring the bell and our grandparents would come out onto the balcony. Only then did I feel that I had truly arrived. The dry heat, so different from the damp Venetian climate, was another proof, together with the red dust that covered the stone floor in the hallway: it was sand blown by the *scirocco* wind all the way from the Sahara. Every year my grandparents would repeat this story and I liked to dream of the sand-clouds drifting through the sky.

Doubt would strike me halfway up the stairs when I reached the statue of the Athenian Lycurgus, who was always wet under his tunic between the legs. It was usually Alessandro, my eldest cousin, who pointed it out to me – so I thought he had done it just before we arrived, as a joke. But even when I passed it by myself, I would always find a dark, damp spot. Sometimes I marvelled at my cousin's perseverance – at other times I found myself wondering whether a statue really could wet itself, especially one of a minister and judicial orator of ancient Greece, inflexible and inexorable, descended from the god Poseidon!

One thing I really miss from Sicily, and from the walks I used to take with my cousin Giandomenico, are *panelle*, a kind of puff pastry made with chick peas and fried in oil. We used to buy them and eat them straight away – because they lose their flavour when cold – at the special shops where the *panellaro* fried them up in a huge pan on a stove made of lava-stone, adding a touch of salt. He started work early in the morning, so that the building workers could get their breakfast of bread and *panelle*. The shape of the thing, a sort of miniature waffle, golden in colour, has given rise to the Sicilian expression '*Pari 'na paniella*' ('It looks like a *panella*'), used for anything that has the misfortune to be crushed under excessive weight. Another saying was: '*Pane e panelle fanno le figlie belle, panelle senza pane fanno una vita da cani*' ('Bread and *panelle* make daughters beautiful, *panelle* without bread make a dog's life'), meaning that if you want to live serenely it's important not to desire only what is superfluous.

Panelle came to Sicily with the Arabs, who ruled the island between the ninth and eleventh centuries. Great gastronomic experimenters, they ground the seeds of the nutritious chick pea plant, which originates in the East, to obtain a kind of flour. When mixed with water and baked, it made a sort of crude pastry, fairly bland in taste. Chick peas are one of the staple

ABOVE: My mother on her way to a
bal en tête, c. 1958.

elements in the diet of the poorer parts of the Mediterranean and are highly prized in Sicily.

Punta Raisi, the airport squeezed beneath Mount Longa and the shore, has never been considered one of the safest. When you take off or land, the nearby Mount Pellegrino looms up to greet you or bid you farewell. In a cave on this mountain is the sanctuary of Santa Rosalia, known as Santuzza, the Protectress of Palermo. The cave contains life-sized wax representations of parts of people's bodies that are claimed to have been cured through the intercession of the saint. Her feast day on 4 September is celebrated with coloured lights, fireworks and devout processions up the mountain to her sanctuary, where the faithful are greeted by vendors of typical Sicilian street food: sweets, *panelle*, pumpkin seeds and calf-spleen sandwiches.

I feel close ties to this land, an island that seems like a continent. Its Mediterranean vegetation is familiar to me, as is the sea that surrounds it and the fishermen who steer their boats southwards, and in my dreams I set off with them towards Africa just across the water, or fly south with the swallows … But when I think of swallows flying, something else comes to mind. *Voli di rondine* (flights of swallows) is the Sicilian way of referring to the sale of family treasures to finance indulgent luxuries, like sending shirts to London to be dry-cleaned and throwing magnificent parties. Such parties are rare now, even though the people are as warm-hearted, hospitable and lively as ever.

Prince Ganci, having accompanied his wife to Paris for her new wardrobe one year, visited Versailles, where the couple fell in love with the Hall of Mirrors and commissioned one just like it for their residence in Palermo. The director Luchino Visconti used it for the ball scene in his film of Lampedusa's novel *The Leopard*, and it took 36 days to film.

In the late nineteenth and early twentieth centuries the Sicilian nobility would regularly visit France and England. The ladies would go to the *haute couture* fashion houses of Paris, the men to London for shirts, made-to-measure shoes and the Gibus – a kind of collapsible top hat made of silk and special springs, invented by a Frenchman, which my grandfather Ciccio always wore. My cousins and I used to play with it like a concertina, or we would imitate my grandfather, wearing it at an angle over our eyes and tucking his bone-handled walking-stick under our arms.

Looking at a photograph, I see my mother reflected in the mirror, numerous mirrors. Those were the days when her brother, my Uncle Franz, who was seven years older, would accompany her to elegant balls given by the Sicilian aristocracy in their magnificent town houses such as the Palazzo Ganci. There she would ascend the grand double flight of marble stairs that led to frescoed salons and listen in fascination to the travellers' tales of the Prince of Ganci, grandfather of little Stefanina Ganci, who was to marry another prince: Vanni Calvello di San Vincenzo. There was no shortage of titles, as in the case of the 80 possessed by the princes Alliata di Villafranca, who still maintain the title of Barons of the Pleasures of Solomon.

My mother was known as 'ninnola' (little doll) to the whole family and was confined to a protected life in the ivory tower of Corso Calatafimi. Yet she still managed to get an insight into the ways of the real world. For a few months one of her 'instructors' was a dazzling cousin – Ninnolo Samonà, one of the many sons of the distinguised architect. It was the period of the EVIS movement – Esercito di Volontari per l'Indipendenza della Sicilia (Volunteer Army for the Independence of Sicily) – and Ninnolo, young and idealistic, had taken part in a demonstration against the Italian state. The group he was with first made their escape over the roofs in the centre of Palermo, and then tried to drive the police away by throwing tiles down at them. Some were caught, including Ninnolo, and taken to the juvenile prison of Malaspina. He stayed there a week before his family managed to get him out and send him into 'exile' at his grand-parents' house. (This was where, by tradition, all grandchildren who had got into any trouble were quarantined.) With a great deal of self-importance and determination he initiated my mother, then aged about ten, into all the tricks of the trade that the petty criminals of old Palermo had taught him during his time as a prison inmate – how to incite pity in passers-by so that they gave you money, then how to pick their pockets afterwards; how to snatch bags on foot or by bicycle; even how to fake a car accident and ask for damages. It was certainly a fine education for a daughter of the Sicilian aristocracy destined to marry into one of Venice's leading families. But then, as I hope I have shown, Italy is always full of surprises.

So now I've reached the end of this journey – travelling through Italy, my country and a land I know so well, I have been struck by its history, traditions, wealth of art and natural beauty. Past and present overlap. Italy has been a beacon of civilization since ancient times and its history offers us marvels and extremes – from the slick glamour of cities in the north through the narrow, winding medieval lanes and eccentric towers in the hill towns to the remote sun-scorched landscapes of Sicily.

Revisiting so much of the country has also encouraged me to reflect on the process of artistic expression. It is interesting that whereas Bramante and Raphael seemed to be concerned with the idea that the arts could converge and blend, Michelangelo felt that the synthesis of art, whether in drawings or in the idea, must remain separate from the material. The ways of expression are limitless, and throughout my journey I have also been able to observe the connection between art and architecture on the one hand, and the sublime natural beauty of this country on the other.

But what has impressed me most has been meeting the Italian people of today, the keepers of this heritage. I found that in their emotions, their language and even their most instinctive behaviour they reflect the wonders of Italy, with a marvellous creativity and *modo di essere*, or way of being. While in a chemist's shop in Naples, I witnessed a touching scene. As she was leaving, an elderly lady wished the pharmacist a good weekend.

He said cordially, 'But we're also open tomorrow.'

'Ah, lovely, so I can pass by and greet you tomorrow as well!'

'Lady,' replied the handsome pharmacist, grinning like a Cheshire cat, 'if it pleases you, just tell me, and *every* Sunday I'll keep the pharmacy open and you can come and greet me.'

CREDITS AND ACKNOWLEDGEMENTS

My family has helped me in every way possible: Jane, my parents Ranieri and Maria Grazia, my mother-in-law Victoria Press, my marvellous children Delia, Vettor and Pierangelo, my brother MarcoAndrea, his wife Tea and sons Alvise and Ranieri, and my Sicilian cousins Alessandro and Giandomenico Vanni d'Archirafi.

As ever, the precious team at BBC Books, including Vivien Bowler, Sarah Reece, Linda Blakemore, Dee O'Reilly and Joanne Forrest Smith, together with Gregory Dowling and Esther Jagger, worked tirelessly to put everything together for this book. John Parker and June Wallis travelled the country to capture the images, and I am grateful for their sensitivity and ideas. The group responsible for the accompanying TV series performed miracles: Roly Keating, Mark Harrison, Basil Comely, Jonty Claypole, Andrea Illescas, Andrea Carnevali, Mike Garner, Dave Williams, Nina Martuccio and Luca Chiari. I have been supported throughout by Laura Hill and Paul Stevens at ICM.

Heartfelt thanks also to the friends I encountered during my travels: Maggie Smith, Giorgio Armani, John Elkann, Lorenzo Rubin de Cervin Albrizzi, Neri Guicciardini, Bettino Ricasoli, his son Francesco and niece Elisabetta Donà dalle Rose, Enzo Zarafa, Bruno Tirell, Ludovico di Valmarana, Marella Caracciolo Chia, Leonardo and Cecilia Lovisatti, Giovanni and Servanne Giol, Mario Icardi and Rocky, his truffle dog, Pepe and Caterina Apuzzo and Gaetano, Beatrice Zardini, Barbara Lippi, Simeone the violinist, Benedetta Origo, Miranda the chef, Martin Clist and Rupert Wace, Edwina Dennison, Manuela Lucà Dazio, Janusz Podrazik and Gioia Meller Marcovicz, Duncan Ward, Gracia Rodriguez Clemente and Stephen Claypole.

I am also grateful to the numerous organizations, nuns and priests that occupy and manage all the buildings and precious collections featured in the documentary series and this book, for opening their doors to us.

BBC Worldwide would like to thank the following for providing photographs and for permission to reproduce copyright material. While every effort has been made to trace and acknowledge copyright holders, we would like to apologize should there have been any errors or omissions.

All of the photographs in this book are © John Parker with the exception of:

Page 45 Bridgeman Art Library/Leonardo da Vinci/Santa Maria della Grazie, Milan, Italy; 54 Corbis/Bob Sacha; 83 left Art Archive/Galleria degli Uffizi, Florence/Dagli Orti; 115 left Corbis/Sandro Vannini; 115 right Private collection, London (courtesy of Rupert Wade Ancient Art); 121 Corbis/Bob Krist; 126 Ettore Majorana Foundation, Sicily; 127 AKG-Images; 133 Corbis/Michael S. Yamashita; 137 Bridgeman Art Library/Buonarroti Michelangelo/Vatican Museums & Galleries, Vatican City, Italy; 139 Bridgeman Art Library/Buonarroti Michelangelo/St Peter's, Vatican, Italy, Giraudon; 154 and 158 Corbis/ John Heseltine; 159 Photolibrary – The Travel Library Ltd; 161 Corbis/Massimo Listri; 162 Art Archive/Archaeological Museum Naples/Dagli Orti; 163 and 164 Corbis/Mimmo Jodice; 166 both and 167 Mary Evans Picture Library; 169 Art Directors/Trip/Tibor Bognar; 173 Corbis/Guenter Rossenbach/zefa; 190 ACI Palermo.
The images on pages 7, 27, 34, 40, 43, 62, 76 left, 83 right, 89, 99 right, 108, 120 and 160 are by Andrea Illescas © BBC.
The images on pages 5 right, 56, 68, 73, 185, 205 below, 208 and 210 were supplied by the author.

We would also like to acknowledge the following for authorizing the reproduction of images of various public sites in Italy, and to thank them for their co-operation and assistance in obtaining them:

Scrovegni Chapel, Padua; Parma Baptistry; Teatro all'Antica, Sabbioneta; Palazzo Te, Mantua; Palazzo Ducale, Urbino; Monreale Cathedral; Palazzo dei Normanni, Palermo; Palazzo Aiutamicristo, Palermo; Cappuccini catacombs, Palermo; Villa Igea, Palermo.

The quotations on pages 102 and 106 have been taken from *The Prince* by Niccolò Macchiavelli, translated by George Bull (Penguin, 1961).

This book is published to accompany the television series entitled *Francesco's Italy: Top to Toe* created by BBC Arts and first broadcast on BBC2 in 2006.
Executive producer: Basil Comely Series producer: Jonty Claypole

Published by BBC Books, BBC Worldwide Limited, Woodlands, 80 Wood Lane, London W12 0TT.

First published 2006
Text © Francesco and Jane da Mosto 2006
The moral right of the authors has been asserted.

ISBN-13: 978 0 563 49348 8
ISBN-10: 0 563 49348 8

Commissioning Editor: Vivien Bowler Project Editor: Sarah Reece
Copy Editor: Esther Jagger Translator: Gregory Dowling
Art Director and Designer: Linda Blakemore Picture Researcher: Joanne Forrest Smith
Cartographer: Alan Burton Production Controller: Kenneth McKay

Set in Bembo, Trajan and Frutiger
Colour origination and printing by Butler & Tanner Limited, Frome, England

For more information about this and other BBC books, please visit our website at www.bbcshop.com or telephone 08700 777 001.

Endpapers: La Foce, Tuscany
Page 2: a reproduction of Michelangelo's statue of David, Piazza della Signoria, Florence
Page 216: a mosaic in the Norman Palace, Palermo, Sicily

INDEX